Here teenagers across Britain, in response to Virago's invitation in *Just Seventeen*, Britain's bestselling teenage magazine, paint a riveting and sobering picture of what life in the eighties means to them. Speaking passionately for themselves, these girls and young women challenge the old adage 'these are the best years of your life'. They show that these may indeed be exhilarating years – of discos and clothes, Live Aid and Madonna – but they are 'no bed of roses', with worries of exams and the dole queue, love and pregnancy, drugs and violence, racism and the Bomb. The writers also show knowing and wry humour, poking fun at their self-confessed obsessions with romance, boys, music and style. Some feel misfits – and angry, some speak with great spirit and strength but admit fear and confusion. Above all, this collection of 'essays from the heart' as BBC Radio One's presenter Janice Long so aptly calls it in her introduction, shows that these teenagers care deeply about having a say in their world. From a wide range of backgrounds, of different races, here are the eighties generation's bitter-sweet dreams.

Lenore Goodings, editor of *Bitter-Sweet Dreams*, was born in Canada in 1953 and came to Britain in 1977. She is Deputy Managing Director of Virago, responsible for publicity and the co-editor of the Virago Upstarts series.

Virago Upstarts is a new series of books for girls and young women. Upstarts are about love and romance, family and friends, work and school – and about new preoccupations – because in the last two decades the lives and expectations of girls have changed a lot. With fiction of all kinds, humour, mystery, love stories, science fiction, detective, thrillers – and nonfiction, this new series will show the funny, difficult, and exciting real lives and times of teenage girls in the 1980s. Lively, down-to-earth and entertaining, Virago's new list is an important new Upstart on the scene.

BITTER-SWEET
DREAMS

Girls' And Young Women's Own Stories
by the readers of

JUST SEVENTEEN

Introduced by Janice Long

Collected by
Lenore Goodings

VIRAGO UPSTARTS

Published by VIRAGO PRESS Limited 1987
41 William IV Street, London WC2N 4DB

British Library Cataloguing in Publication Data

Bitter-sweet Dreams : Girls' and young
women's own stories.—(Virago upstarts)
1. Youth—Great Britain
941.085′8′0922   HQ799.G7

ISBN 0-86068-913-1

Typeset by Florencetype Ltd, Kewstoke, Avon
Printed in Great Britain
by Cox & Wyman Ltd of Reading, Berkshire

CONTENTS ◀

Introduction by *Janice Long*

For my sister Laurel,
whose teenage years I missed

ACKNOWLEDGEMENTS

It has to be said that this book is a group effort – not least because it has forty-six contributors. I want to thank first of all the girls and young women who responded so enthusiastically to our notice in *Just Seventeen* magazine. It was an illuminating and exhilarating chance to find out at first hand what hundreds of teenagers think about their lives. Thanks too to Wendy Varley and Bridget LeGood at *Just Seventeen* for their co-operation. Enormous and grateful thanks are due to Charlotte Greig for helping me with editing. John Annette encouraged me and for the inspiration and the idea, I thank Melanie McFadyean.

L.G.

INTRODUCTION BY JANICE LONG

It wasn't that long ago that 'teenage' books were written by doctors, educationalists and the like – establishment figures with text book ideas. The danger with these books was that if you didn't fit in with their theories, you were made to feel odd. To me, the only valid words, thoughts and opinions of girls and young women are their own.

So great! A book is published; forty-six of you have contributed to it, about 70,000 words in all. But this is only a start.

Even though it seems that the controllers of the media are waking up to the idea that public access makes for real communication, when were students seriously asked about the education system? When did programme makers ever consult you and act upon it? When did an often male and middle-aged medical profession show real concern about your body? And why is it that parents always forget everything they went through as kids? If everybody remembered what they felt like ten years ago then our problems would be appreciated and not ignored.

Comparing hopes and fears and bitter-sweet dreams must be very comforting if only to realise that you are not the only one who is, for example, scared by what the future holds. While it is reassuring to feel that others too, don't know what love is, or how to talk to a boyfriend, or dread unemployment, or have nightmares about the Bomb, it is not enough. To really change things, these essays from the heart need to be read and reacted to by the very groups of people who are at the root of these problems.

So read the book and then get your friends, sisters, brothers (especially brothers!), parents and teachers to read it. Encourage debate and discussion and let's have a whole series of books, and not in a 'minority' category but in the mainstream. Let's see regular columns in popular papers, and teenage magazines written by teenagers (well done *Just Seventeen*), teenagers on radio shows, T.V. shows, and maybe even a teenage minister in parliament. She should actually be under twenty-one!

But we have not yet arrived, and one book does not make a social revolution. We must not stop here. We must battle to have more say in decisions which affect our lives.

London, 1987

GOOD TIMES ◄

HILARY EDWARDS

Wirral, Merseyside

Sometimes, I think it would be better and safer to skip teenage years and just jump straight into adult life, where people will take notice of what you want to say. As an adult, your views can be heard and you can't be as easily hurt by other people. If you're fourteen, like me, you're a nothing. You may be classed as a 'teenager' by society, but by your family, your school and your teachers you're thought of more as a kid who has just embarked on puberty.

Things are changing; we know a lot more now than we ever did and half of it comes from magazines – learning about your body and sex, that is. Parents are coming out of their shells more and a lot more talking is going on in families like mine. We can talk about anything in our family and we rarely get embarrassed about it, but some are different. I once had a friend who, when she started her periods, just couldn't face telling her mum. She cried about it and used loo paper – until we found out. We gave her our stuff but we never found out when she did tell her mum. The funny thing was, she was rock hard. Her mum had remarried and she went through some rough patches with her new dad. She had two brothers and a sister that were younger than her and she took care of them like a second mother, advising them, telling them off. But she couldn't face something like a period – it just cracked her up.

But most bits of being a teenager are great fun. You get more responsibility and can go out more. You meet boys, a major step in every young girl's life. No more kiss-chase in the playground – this is the real stuff! You get your first tongue sarnie! Hurrah! Some don't, of course; these are the

3

ones that never get hurt by boys, never get drunk, never rip their best skirt and go into a depression, the ones who don't get into as much trouble as the average party-goer. These teenagers may wish they could be like the girl-next-door, while the girl-next-door may wish she is the one that passes all her exams, gets a good job and settles down with a devoted husband who gives her two angelic kids.

I started a diary a couple of days ago because I didn't want to forget my younger life. I don't want to grow old and lose my memory and get cataracts. People don't respect you at all if you're old, you get written off because you've had your little fling in life and now you can get lost and fade into the background. You wonder if they ever got into serious trouble for coming home too late, or if they had a dream of becoming famous.

What am I going to turn into? Sometimes I get dead worried about not getting a job. I'd really love to act – I'm good at that, but will producers and directors think so? Let's face it, tons of people want to act and they're all older and better than me, so who's going to give me a chance? So I turn to working hard at school in the hope that I'll get a job in medicine, knowing quite well that my personality's going to be wasted in a stuffy hospital. I love messing about and getting attention, but I can't afford to make a career out of it.

But if you're not careful, you get disillusioned about life. You read magazines and photo stories: you drop something, a Mr Perfect picks it up for you, flashes a pearly grin and Hey Presto! You've got it made! Wrong again. Love is the pits and it just doesn't happen like that. Some magazines print stories about girls who didn't get many 'O' levels, left school and started their own businesses because they make a mean piece of jewellery. What happened to the story about the lad who, likewise, didn't get many 'O' levels, left school, went on the dole and got so depressed he committed suicide? When you discover the truth, it's a shock at the price of twenty-five pounds a week on a YTS.

So what is there left for the average teenager? Some friends of mine do drugs and spend their days either stoned, drunk or running from the police. And me? I'm just a fourteen-year-old Little Miss Nobody who goes to school, works hard and dreams about becoming an actress. Whatever happened to the swinging sixties, please? A time of love, peace and acc music. Well, people, these are the swinging eighties, a time of nuclear bombs, doped-up kids and racism. Congratulations! This is the real world and you're welcome to it.

MICHELLE MURPHY

Northfield, West Midlands

Well, let's start off with the dictionary's view of a Teenager: 'A young person thirteen to nineteen years old.' Personally, I believe that leaves a lot to be desired. It is not even a whole sentence.

So who are these people, these thirteen- to nineteen-year-olds? Is that all we know about them? What is their function in society, what do they look like, how do they dress, how do they smell, etc? But, most of all we need to know, is it true that their only interest in life is a dog-like interest in sex?

Well, I can start to make these points clear to you by introducing myself on the scene. Here is a real-life teenager. Though an ageing one to be blunt, for I am all of sixteen years old. A terrifying age, I might add. It is only fair for me to explain sixteen-year-olds as I do not really understand the older or younger teenagers. In fact, I do not really understand sixteen-year-olds very well, but I do understand me. So here we go.

I am a bit Irish, a bit Scottish and mostly English. Thus my Gaelic looks, my stingy character and my writing to you. I am the best of eight, in other words, the last child. I am slightly spoilt and extremely mature. One of my sisters is extremely loopy, the maddest of us all (she gets it off my mother, who is also that way inclined). I have four sisters and three brothers and I live above a rest-home for the elderly. Do I need to continue? Yes, I do.

Well, I now want to introduce my brother Thomas. He is twenty-seven at the moment and lives in Nottingham. He is important, because since I first joined the ranks of those thirteen- to nineteen-year-olds, I have been visiting him while he is at university. Most of my teenage years so far have been spent commuting between Birmingham and Nottingham, to enjoy the student life with my brother. Ah, I hear you say, this girlie leads a double life! Well, that is one way of putting it. You see, whenever I had any exams at school, I used to skip off to Nottingham basically to avoid them, while growing into my fake student skin.

I used to get quite confused; then I would return definitely older and wiser, but only to slip back into my childish ways. All very stimulating stuff. So here I sit today in my virgin white room that is partly covered with black and white pictures. I mostly write poems and plan my attack on the world of photography here. Yes, that is in between doing my 'O' levels. You see for the past three years, I have been perfecting my literary talents, as well as my ideas for my fame in photos. I lust so strongly for future fame that purely on strength of that alone I shall stun the art world. I have nothing to lose, that is why I send poems to mags, so

6

that even if they do not publish them, I shall have the satisfaction in future years when I am being interviewed by *The Face* etc, to say, 'Well, folks, you had your chance when I was a mere babe and boy, did you mess it up! Ha Ha.' Ooh, it makes me all prickly with eagerness; so beware wild old world, this sixteen-year-old is out to get you and you can either grab me while I am hot or try it when I am burning up.

So what of this sixteen-years-of-age terrifying bit? Well, now I am sixteen I am slightly more responsible for my pitiful actions. Also, when I visit my brother in Notts now he is viciously protective, or so I found on my last visit. I ponder on this. He never showed concern before, always let me get out of my own mess. It is almost a regression. I mean when I was fifteen, he did not mind who I snogged. But suddenly he has got prickly. It's quite nice, really, I think it is because perhaps he realises that I am a much more viable proposition these days.

Now for a little poem:

Through the dim light of dawn I wake
Freezing cold begin to shake
Turn me upside down and what do you imagine you see
It is still me yes me
I am new and crisp a breath of fresh air
Slightly scented over skimming mountains and valleys I
   skip to dare
Youth has little to lose and plenty to learn
Oh but I am no fool I will know old age when it creeps
When I put on lipstick without looking at my lips
Then I am lost and rightly so
Another will come bounding through the snow.

My version of youth for you there!

ANONYMOUS

Gillingham, Kent

For me being a teenager in the eighties is a good experience. I come from a good home, have loving parents, a nice house to live in, my own room and a sister to talk to. The area I live in has many facilities for people my age; there is the 'Ice Bowl', a new skating rink, and in Chatham, the nearest town to us, there are three swimming pools and the Regency (the local disco). But that's my world, my slice of cake. It's not the same 'outside'.

The eighties are different to other decades in many ways. Young people are the key to it – the key to its problems, but we're not the ones to blame, we're the victims. The government is causing lack of jobs, drug-pushers are pushing drugs to the helpless, and people blame the youth for violence, but it is because young people are depressed because of these problems that they turn violent. Besides the problems though, there is another view. There are good things in the eighties.

I believe that one day we will be known and remembered because of our uniqueness and the way we are always changing. There's clothes: unlike the sixties or the seventies we don't have a set fashion of any sort. We do our own thing. There are hundreds of different types of clothes selling in the shops and we can be as outrageous as we like without getting ridiculed or laughed at. There's our pop groups, which die out as quickly as they become known. Everything around us is changing and unless you learn to change with it, you're left behind.

Teenagers can express themselves much more easily now. Nothing is being kept from us anymore. It's all being revealed. Sex is openly spoken about. So are other things

8

like violence. We are all being warned now to be careful, to watch out for all the dangers of life. Teenagers are developing their own opinions. We are beginning to have some say in what's being done to *our* world. Marriage, voting, homosexuality, the Pill, smoking, all these subjects are now being discussed and thought about by us. Most of the time, these things are discussed in school; nothing comes out of it, but at least we are allowed to voice our thoughts. This is definitely helping us, as many problems are caused by lack of communication.

I have just told you about the differences of the eighties compared to any other decade, but many of these don't affect me in my sheltered corner of the world. My life is centred around eating, sleeping, school, ice-skating and boys. In a way you could say that my friends and I are blissfully unaware of our world, despite the fact that we live in it. Every day we wake up and it's there, so we ignore it. At thirteen, I suppose that's acceptable. We don't have much to worry about. No 'O' levels or 'A' levels for years yet. No hunting for jobs. The real teenager of sixteen or seventeen isn't really a teenager for much longer; if they can't find a job, they have all the responsibilities of adulthood launched on them. Money's tight – you can't fritter it away on enjoying yourself. At that age, it's unjust, you *should* be able to enjoy yourself.

My views, my emotions, my likes, my dislikes, my ambitions are all to do with the media. I've been influenced by them and by books. I believe that they have probably got more control over people than the government. They are my entrance to the outside world, I can find through them what's really happening. I don't often like what I find out though, like the rapes which we keep hearing about, or the grotesque murders of small children. There is obviously more violence now, which worries me and my friends.

9

The arms race also causes us concern. It's something most teenagers don't like to talk about.

The eighties are like a breakthrough point for us; we're starting to get treated like adults. Everything is faster now, you do things at an earlier age. Girls and boys first go out together at twelve years, some try out smoking at twelve and some first have sex at fourteen or fifteen. You first start going out late at night with your friends at twelve, providing your parents collect you. It's now considered OK to wear make-up, to drink, to smoke, to go out with boys, to go to the cinema and see a fifteen-rated film, when you are only thirteen. It doesn't matter if you upset anyone doing these things. It's to hell with rules, as everyone has a non-conformist attitude.

You don't work at school, you just mess around. Yet, mysteriously, most people still get good marks in exams. You go crazy over pop stars and fight over posters with your sister. You help run up your parents' phone bill and disappear when 'work' is mentioned. Your room's always in a mess. The walls can't be seen for posters. There's always music blaring away. You're constantly getting into debt with other members of your family so that you can go out, and never stop nagging your mum for that pair of shoes you saw in the shops. Everything's funny, you laugh about sex, clothes, your friends' hair, and are constantly bitching behind each other's backs. You know every detail about each other. Each boy you go out with counts as another medal to add to your collection. You have two vocabularies – one you use at home and one when you are with your friends. You rarely read books unless they have scenes in considered worth hiding from your mum. You always walk a certain way to the local shopping centre past the walls of someone's back garden so that you can catch up on the latest graffiti and add some of your own. If whilst you're out shopping a fight (a scrap, really) starts you make sure you get a good view – right at the front until someone breaks it up.

This is my life as a teenager of the eighties. I'm sure that many people can identify with it. Next year, my sister becomes a teenager and the cycle of finding out for yourself on how to spend your teenage years will begin for her.

LAURI OWENS

Nailsea, Avon

On Monday

Seeming vaguely nervous at first,
I do not think it matters. I pick up the pace.
I race. At last, I wear the devil's hat.
So what, my bosoms are enormous. Monumental.
These are things of glory.
Breathing sexuality in jaded fullness
Ostentatiously ignoring every horn.
Hard-core, sprayed on, tousled porn.
Bangles jangle, lashes spill,
yes, love, my face is plastered to the hilt.
Mile high spikes advance a trollop's tilt.
Ass out, stomach in, the Whore of Babylon's sister Sin.
My womankin do not appreciate the line,
looking constipated left or right –
never in the eyes of this wanton sight.
Reflecting Man's view of magnificence,
white slave with overflowing cup.
Jeez, some days I do so enjoy sending both sides up.

11

KATIE BLADES

Kelsale, Suffolk

Hayley got off her bed and glanced in the mirror. She glossed her lips, encircled her eyes in black liner, careful not to smudge it along the lid, taking it out as far as possible on the outer corner. Hurriedly, she backcombed her browny-gold, treacle-coloured, dyed hair and tied it with black lace. Hayley looked up to see how closely she resembled her idol. Madonna's eyes glowed back; even on a poster they looked alive, fiery, full of fun. She looked at the other pop posters: Billy Idol, Marc Almond, Depeche Mode and Prince, stuck haphazardly with Blu-Tack on the white (not quite) walls. It was an odd selection of pop stars, neither one way or the other, which matched Hayley's musical taste. She wasn't into what she termed really meaningful, deeply depressing, semi-political arty music, such as Talk Talk, The Smiths, Talking Heads and The Cult, yet she wasn't a teenybopper escapist – these days it seemed nobody was. The music had died. Spandau Ballet had become but a dim memory of rock and pop awards ceremonies. Despite their appearance in Live Aid even Duran Duran were fading, still pop stars, but drifting into other things. Now, the end of the duo which had for the past two years been the epitome of teenybopper idealism: Wham! had split up after a five-hour farewell performance at Wembley, (Hayley would have gone, had she been able to get tickets). But still she couldn't deny that it wasn't so long ago that she'd been through a total Wham! phase. Even those who professed to hate them had to admit that George Michael was a very talented singer and songwriter, as well as being good-looking (in an obvious sort of way).

Hayley was somewhere in the middle, she liked dance music but hated electro, felt passionate about A-Ha but also liked The Core. It was confusing, because it wasn't just music, it was everything else as well. She wasn't a Sloane or a hippy, a casual, or any one of the extremes: mod, punk, Greebo. Yet she had friends on both sides, even some Sharons and Kevins, casuals of the white socks, bleach-blond flicked hair, sling-backs and block-pleat, slit-skirt brigade. She felt some alliance with every culture.

Every year when she saw the mods and scooterists go past towards Yarmouth on Easter Bank holiday, it enlivened her interest in them; at these times, like everyone else, she thought of becoming one. There were several at her school, and yet how could she? She'd recently suffered the barbs of some fourth-year modettes, who seemed to be the nearest the school had to feminists and expressed total disapproval of her bare midriff, excessive jewellery and lace. Anyway around where she lived, boys with scooters (Vespas and Lambrettas) seemed hard to come by, and as graduating to Scooter Girl was every modette's ambition the boyfriend was an essential requirement, just as the ghetto blaster was to the breaker.

Hayley sometimes wondered if she was of any one subculture. Sometimes it seemed important, sometimes not. Right now, Hayley was really into the Madonna look, even though it got a mixed reaction (and the original's image had already changed again, perhaps more since Madonna's marriage); but Hayley liked it. It was outrageous, imaginative, rebellious, feminine and tough at the same time. It gave her the freedom of being able to mix with other cults like punks while still allowing her own identity because it wasn't a subculture but a style.

The clique to which Hayley now belonged were not lookalikes exactly, more clones. They followed the basic ideas, and then adapted and customised the look to suit themselves. That's why there were 'true followers' and 'fakers'. The latter just put on their style to go out in, whereas 'true followers' lived their lives by style. Hayley was one of these. She'd never have discussed it with any of the others, you just knew who was and wasn't, you could pick them out in the street and they in return would acknowledge you.

Hayley was now sitting, just staring around her room. There were other pictures too, some of cherished importance to her generation: James Dean, Marilyn Monroe and, strangely enough, Marlon Brando. There were pictures of other actors too, mostly members of the Brat Pack (America's young eligibles – Tom Cruise, Matt Dillon, Rob Lowe, etc). Hayley's favourites were actually Sean Penn, Eddie Kid and Aidan Quinn, for obvious reasons.

On her table was a small bag, pink in colour. It was not a handbag, she made a point of letting everyone know that she wasn't a handbag type of person. Handbag people had boyfriends called Gary or John, and friends called Tracey, because usually they were called Sharon and wore slingbacks in the same plastic and colour as their handbag and numerous accessories: belt, earrings, necklace, bangles, all in a lurid shade of green, blue or red, most likely contrasted with pastels or white (or, in winter, grey). Handbag people were second generation casuals, who wore clothes exactly as chainstore manufacturers intended them to be worn.

Eventually, Hayley stood up, got her new black shiny jacket out of the wardrobe (her parents had said no to a leather) and picked up a pair of red lace gloves. It took her

14

a few minutes more to locate her personal stereo (she hated the word Walkman) and then she bounced out of her room and down the stairs with 'Manic Monday' jangling in her ears.

JACQUIE BLOESE

Vale, Guernsey

I remember well my first disco, a typical first experience, I expect. It was held at the neighbouring boys' grammar school – all correct and above board – no smoking, no drinking. My mother approved. My naiveness shone out through my feeble and conventional attempts at fashion – the blue eyeshadow, pink cheeks, pink ra-ra skirt and matching handbag. Yes, a true teenybopper. I remember us laying our crisp pound notes down before a 'hip' teacher in the foyer, all blue jeans and grubby T-shirt. Then we hung sheepishly around the door, behind which came the tantalising sounds of the beat. The inevitable squabbles arose.

'You go in first.'

'No, why should I?'

'You're older than me.'

'So what?'

'Oh, let's walk in together!'

The door was pushed open and we stepped tentatively inside. We found seats and stayed rooted to them, petrified for the first hour. Then we relaxed, bought Cokes, giggled over the boys, even danced – in a huge circle. The barriers were broken down and by the end of the evening we felt like old hands. We looked down our noses at our juniors;

suddenly they seem so very immature. We were invincible, we were rebels, all we cared about was going out. Down with homework, down with fuddy-duddy parents; and with this comforting thought, we were driven home to our electric blankets and cups of Horlicks.

It's the people that make a place, whatever anyone would have you believe, not the music, the DJ, the flashlighting or the decor. What is so intriguing about a load of run-of-the-mill kids, all enclosed in the same room? It's not particularly interesting, if we're being honest. No famous faces or millionaires here.

In a disco there is always a perfect place to be stationed, which invariably is occupied. These occupants are the first in line for surveillance. They are known as the *hardened clubbers* – you know the type. The majority have left school and if they haven't, they're too tired to attend full time anyway. They devote their lives to obtaining tickets for every disco or party going. They are usually sprawled casually across the chairs. Occasionally, they exchange a few words with the DJ or receive a namecheck over the microphone in the guise of a joke. On hearing the first couple of beats of a chart-song they rise, before anyone else has even registered the suitability of the song to dance to. They dance, monotonously but faultlessly, their steps scarcely missing a beat, in perfect timing. They are oblivious to those about them – they know the dance floor and the record so intimately that they know exactly when to add those small but necessary touches to their repertoire. They are like sleepwalkers, totally unselfconscious. How could they possibly be otherwise? They come here at every possible opportunity. The moment the record ends they return to their seats – no lingering like fools on the dance floor waiting for the assurance of the DJ that the record has indeed finished.

They exchange casual small talk, similar to that a group of close friends might have over coffee. Occasionally they may stifle a yawn or wipe a bleary eye. They've no time for eight hours' sleep and all that rubbish. Life is one long party – intercepted briefly and cruelly by work.

Let us move around the room a little to the *trendies*. A select, sparse mixture of young people. Girls have geometric cropped hairstyles with brash make-up. Boys have medium to long hair, gelled and streaked. The boys sport brightly-coloured shirts and casual trousers, patterned in subtle colours. Girls are also in bright colours and are not dressed for the heat – swamped in polo necks, leggings, miniskirts galore. Their talk is bright and eager as is their energetic dancing to the recently released records hovering outside the charts. They sometimes cast swift, snide glances at fellow dancers, wondering how they can be so 'out'. These glances are countered with bitchy whispers and forced laughter. These people are usually in the 'in' place, although they tend to acquaint themselves with varied nightspots so that everyone can have the chance to see how totally fashionable they are.

Move towards the bar and you'll see a substantial amount of people, who, nine times out of ten, will be screaming with false laughter or generally drawing attention to themselves. These are the *clones*. The girls have permed shoulder-length hair, a brightly coloured top belted over a straight skirt. Immaculate. How can we be criticised they say indignantly? We're wearing fashionable clothes, look – here's the chain store label. Our clothes match our shoes and earrings – we're good dancers. Our interests – A-Ha and 'Eastenders' of course. We go out at least twice a week, Friday and Saturday usually – with our boyfriends if we've got one at the time but if not we go out with our mates. We have a good laugh – what more could anyone ask?

The room is dark but on closer observation you will discover that a corner of it is swamped in black. What is it you ask? A rather dodgy lighting system? An area conveniently set aside for those who prefer more discreet passionate clinches, away from prying eyes and wagging tongues? No, these are the freaks/gothic punks/individuals, whichever they prefer to label themselves as. Cooler than the Siberian winter, moodier than Morrissey, these kids have a tough time. What with the older generation breathing down their necks and their generation dubbing them weird – it's not easy being an original. Wait – here comes an old Cure number – great, it's really depressing! Mustn't get too enthusiastic though – smiling just doesn't suit the deathly white pallor. They drift zombie-like onto the dance floor – in shapeless black flowing garments. Females – light black shirts and a Marks & Spencer's V-neck. Half a ton of crosses and chains can be a terrible strain, so heads are bowed and bodies sway emotively with a serious waving of the arms and fingers. Giving a contemptuous glance at the bright spark who is imitating them, to the amusement of the onlookers, boys and girls alike continue to gyrate on an otherwise deserted dance floor. Boys invariably have a cigarette somewhere on their person, be it in the corner of the mouth, behind the ear, or between the fingers and waved about creating a fine mist of smoke – cosmic man! By this time, by popular demand from the majority, the DJ removes the song which now thoroughly resembles a funeral dirge and replaces it with a bright boppy number from Wham! and the floor fills again.

An air of relief prevails as the visions in black return disgusted to their corner to smoke and plan their outing *en masse* to the graveyard later on. People pick on us because we're individuals, they lament. We do our own thing, we dress how we want – why should we conform?

We have only touched the surface of the types of nationally approved disco-goers. Of course there are numerous other varieties, for example the tart and the poser. But doubtless most people go to a disco falsely secure in the knowledge that they are normal, typical and happy. Discos are about releasing tension and enjoyment. The disco is an excuse to come out of yourself, a place to be seen in, a place in which to talk and to be talked about. Our parents had no such privilege, the future generations will probably mock discos and progress to places of increased sophistication. Meanwhile teenagers world-wide continue to line the pockets of the club bosses and, in return, are provided with a chunk of teenage life, which will remain in the memory, revived occasionally in later years as a sweet reminder of youth in the 1980s.

JOANNE GREENHALGH

South Croydon, London

Life in the eighties has been full of ups and downs: drugs, child abuse, royal weddings, Wispas, *Just Seventeen*, abortions, the Pill, young mothers, I could go on. No doubt many people will be able to write with much inspiration on one or many other topics of the eighties, but Sport Aid is something that made me really sit and think. I think I shall remember the eighties as a good era; no doubt, as in other eras, there were many traumas (nuclear weapons, etc), but think how much good has come also from the eighties.

Obviously, there was not just Sport Aid, but Live Aid

19

and Fashion Aid, but I never really participated in these other events. I bought the record 'Do they know it's Christmas?' along with thousands of others, but I failed to actually take part until Sport Aid.

When I did, never have I felt such a sense of community, a crowd of people all aiming for the same thing, to complete the race, enjoy it and raise lots of money for the starving children. Every little detail and event that day was captured in my mind for life. The tube was my means of transport and that of millions of others too; our bodies were strung together, clinging on to keep our balance. The throng of people getting off at the destination moved slowly together, towards the exit like a snake. The atmosphere was ecstatic, everyone was hyped up. On seeing the event later on television, I realised how much atmosphere was missed out on TV. This made me realise that children of the future will never be able to actually feel the tremendous atmosphere. It is this thought that made me put pen to paper.

Normally I am the watcher, the bystander, but not that day; I was in the race, participating. Everyone was happy, beaming faces were such a sight that day that I wondered if we were all receiving energy from each other. The morale boost and feeling of everyone smiling was incredible. In a perfect world, people would be like this all the time. Try to imagine thousands and thousands of people clapping to the noise of car hooters, try to imagine people singing together as a mass, imagining and believing is reality. A boy was carrying a ghetto blaster with the Top Forty pouring out into the frenzied London streets, and thousands of people were singing along with the pop stars. Picture a man standing on top of a letter box, with a camera, he shouts 'smile' and in return, thousands smile and wave back at him. A couple waving from a balcony are received by the crowds like royalty, as thousands wave back to them.

The start of the race: the countdown. People positioned all over Hyde Park, thousands queuing to start. A child's ball is thrown in the air, a mass of people play volleyball back and forth with it. Thousands cheering, singing and applauding. Human pyramid competitions take place, and the crowds enthusiastically roar and scream approval.

We were one, running for a cause. The eighties may be remembered for many bad things, but the good things such as Sport Aid showed just how much people cared and wanted to help.

'We are the World.' How true. The world ran for a need, a need that should never be forgotten. Sport Aid, with the others, should have its own place in the history books, because we made history, as a world united for a starving country.

YOUNG ◀ MOTHERHOOD

ANNMARIE MAGUIRE

Belfast

I left school when I was fourteen, or rather, they threw me out. I was caught smoking and wearing white socks. White socks may not seem like a great crime but, you see, the socks weren't part of the uniform. Besides they wanted to be rid of me anyway. And I suppose I was happy enough to go. I had spent the last year in 'tutorials', which is what they did to you if they didn't like you. They put us in a plain big room where they gave us kids' jigsaws and the like, the kind of work you'd give primary school kids. They tried to humiliate us, while us with the 'problems' wondered who really had the problems.

If you did anything wrong in 'tutorials', the next step was the Green Room. That was a room with four stark green walls, boarded-up windows and a dim light. I think it was designed to drive you mad, like some invention from the Middle Ages. Finally, like all the others who were giving the system bother, I ended up in the Green Room when I couldn't take any more of the jigsaws and other educational inventions. That was enough for me. I told them I wasn't staying, that I was going on home. The teacher said that if I got up to move, she'd lock the door. I heard one of the head teachers coming and I said, 'Can I get out of here?' Then she started, so I just walked on home. The next day, when I went back to school, they told me not to come back. At the time, all sorts of people from the school board were supposed to come chasing me up, but they never bothered. Maybe it was because I lived in West Belfast where these things aren't all that important. A lot of other girls ended up the same way – all expelled for stupid little things, simply because the teachers couldn't cope with the classes.

In work I haven't had much luck either. There is no work really. Where I live – Ballymurphy – 87 per cent of the people are unemployed. It's always been like that. Even in the early seventies when there was full employment, 47 per cent of the people here couldn't get a job. That was because the Unionists controlled everything and made sure that no work ever came into nationalist areas. As well as that, I couldn't have got a job anyway as I was only fourteen and had no cards. And you had to be sixteen to get into a Youth Training Scheme. Although that would hardly have done much good with no jobs around anyway. So for two years I had nothing to do at all. I couldn't even sign on the dole. Then, at last, I was sixteen, and could start looking for a job. But, after one short experience I became pregnant and that was the end of that.

The job I had was in the local Leisure Centre. That was cheap labour. I got £25 a week for working from nine in the morning to nine or ten at night. Cooking, cleaning, serving, keeping the canteen going. I was left to run it myself. It was very, very rare that the others came near me. I had to open up in the morning and lock up at night – twelve hours a day, four days a week, all for a lousy £25 a week. It was around Christmas that, as I said, I became pregnant, just when I might have got a more reasonable seasonal job. But it turned out to be a good thing for me.

You see, I had had terrible trouble with my ovaries. I had been in and out of hospital a couple of times and they had told me that there was a chance that later in life I wouldn't be able to have children. So my boyfriend and I thought it was as well to go ahead now. Mummy and Daddy knew after the operation – that's when they said that there was a possibility of the tubes being blocked – that Joey and me were going to go on ahead.

Then one night we were out. I was drinking Coke all

26

night and I got big pains in my stomach. I didn't know what it was and was rushed down to hospital. I had been panicking, feeling all the pains and that, and not wanting to go to the hospital in case something serious was wrong. That's when they showed me the scan – I was only ten weeks then – and they showed me the wee heartbeat and all. It was great. Seeing the wee life inside. But for the nine months I was afraid of something going wrong.

Nothing went wrong, and I now have a 'full time job' that I love more than anything in my life. Sometimes now I wonder what Belfast will be like when my daughter grows up. Will the Troubles still be going on? All my own life they're all I remember, it's all I've ever known. I was only one year old when it all started, just a wee bit older than my own baby; that was when the Orangies burned us out of Excise Street. That was the start of it. My first birthday – not that I can remember it – was spent with my parents trying to get us away from the Orangies. Then it just went on from that, moving from house to house to house. My mother is twenty-two years married, and we've had twenty-one houses, and in one of the houses we lived for seven years, so some of them have been only for three or six months – time to get it wallpapered and settle in and make new friends, and then away we went again.

It was because of my daddy really. He was on the run from the Brits. And once they found out where we lived we had to move on again, because they kept raiding the house looking for him. In the end he was interned without trial. Then a few years later he was jailed for IRA activities. He's been a prisoner of war for six years now and he has another two years to go. It's going to be very hard for him when he gets out. When you think of it, he had five kids when he went in, and they were all young. Now two of them are married, and by the time he gets out, I expect I'll have a place of my own too. And Kathleen, my younger sister, will be fifteen and probably going steady and getting ready to go her own way. So there will only be two kids left in the house. He'll have missed out on all of us growing up, especially Martin, the youngest, who was only six months old when he was arrested. He's also got four grandchildren now that he hasn't a clue about. He doesn't know *us*, his own kids, never mind his grandchildren. But I expect he'll get closer to them in the long run than to us, because he'll probably see them growing up – what he missed with all of us. It's really sad when you think about it that way. Belfast does that to families.

But, in spite of the war, it's not a bad place to live. I haven't really lived anywhere else, but two years ago I was in Berlin for a few weeks on an exchange visit, representing the management of our local resource centre. (I am a member of the centre's Young Women's Group.) In Berlin, I missed the closeness of here. People walked by one another in the street as if the others didn't exist. It was like a big, busy no-man's-land. Up here, you meet people all the time. People are friendly and helpful to one another. Although nobody is well off, with everyone on the dole and that, there's still a lot of happiness here. I wouldn't really want to leave.

I don't have many ambitions now, I'm too busy with the wee one. But I would like to get a place of my own and that's very hard. There's just too many people looking for houses and all the nationalists have been squeezed into West Belfast. I'd like a Saturday job too. I wouldn't want to work full time, but a few hours a week would be good. It would give Joey the chance to spend time on his own with our daughter Aine – that's her name. However, I myself wouldn't want to spend too much time away from her. After trying so hard against so many odds, I want to be able to spend as much time as possible with her. I wouldn't want to leave her now.

And Belfast just goes on as it always has.

ANONYMOUS

West Midlands

I'm a teenager of eighteen. My teenage years haven't been as good as they could have been, they are over now in a way because I have a son; I'm an unmarried mother.

By the time my five-month-old son is capable of looking after himself I'll be thirty-four years old, too old to do things that I am now missing out on.

I would love to go to nightclubs and be like other people my age enjoying themselves; I'll never have these things but it's my own fault, I should have taken something to stop myself getting pregnant.

Since my teenage days, I've had two long relationships with boys. The first lasted three years but we were never really serious and we had nothing at all in common. I was too young to go to pubs and terrified of getting pregnant (not that my mum would have minded, it's nothing different in the eighties, everybody seems to have babies).

I got pregnant by my second boyfriend. He didn't want the baby but I wouldn't have an abortion. I was too scared. My boyfriend wouldn't marry me, he wanted to be free (these were the very words he said). He didn't want to listen to a screaming baby day in and day out. I got used to the idea after a while and I couldn't wait to put the clothes I'd bought on the baby; my boyfriend bought him nothing at all.

I never really thought about what it would be like to stay in every night while I was pregnant, I was so used to going out five nights a week. He's born now and I do love him, but I do wish that I was still free. Before I was pregnant I worked as a hairdresser. I hated the job at the time but now I think what a good job it was; I wish I could do it again. I'll never be a professional hairdresser now, it was something I always wanted to be. If I had the choice to go back in time I would and I'd make sure I didn't get pregnant this time. I would have a baby when I was married, but I'd want to be at least twenty-eight years old.

I read in magazines about girls getting pregnant or having affairs or something similar. Years ago things like this didn't happen; if you got pregnant you would have to get married. So the eighties have been terrible years for girls being raped or young children being murdered. Quiet, decent lives shouldn't be so full of violence and fear. I never go out of my home without a knife. My friends think it's silly to carry one because they don't think anything will happen to them or me, but that's what everyone thinks. I don't take any chances, those sort of men wouldn't care if you were pushing a baby around in a pram, they'd still rape you and kill the child. Men's minds are vulgar, the world would be a better place without them.

It's television that causes it. Nearly every programme you see is about sex or violence, it gives people ideas. Worst of all are videos. You can get really dirty ones from a video shop for about a pound. Men can't put up with just watching them, they like to go and try the things out on decent people. The number of rapes in the eighties has been the highest ever – the same years videos came out.

I don't know what the world will be like in a couple of years' time. Let's all hope it doesn't get worse. At least I'm glad my baby boy wasn't a girl, for obvious reasons. For

30

women, life is hell no matter what age you are. If you're old you get mugged and beat up. Old people are too weak to help themselves. As I grow old I'll try hard to protect myself, when I'm too old I'll put myself in an old people's home, at least you're safe in there.

No girl or woman is safe to walk the streets alone. I've had a man expose himself to me. It really scared me, this is the main reason I carry a knife around. I can't understand what a man gets from life doing this. But if I was with a friend at the time I wouldn't have been scared. I'd have laughed at him and remarked about it.

Drugs are another reason rape or violence happens. They seem to be sold everywhere and teenagers are dying of drugs each day. Most people have them to be like their friends and they think they look good. But they can't do anything about it once they're addicted. These people end up having no friends or family to be with. They become depressed and usually kill themselves.

I went to Spain two years ago, drugs were being smoked by loads of people and sold. Even owners of pubs were smoking it. I would never touch the stuff but I did get into a drinking habit over there. They served me alcohol and they could tell I was too young. Since I went, I drink all the while now. I'm not an alcoholic, nowhere near that point, but I drink to feel calm mainly. I never get drunk. I also smoke a lot, about twenty fags a day. I started when I was at school because my friends did. I wish I'd never started now, it takes all my money away and I know it's making my health bad, but I can't stop now.

I'm unemployed, like thousands of people in England. I have to save very hard for clothes for myself and the baby, even his clothes are expensive. I get a bit of money off the father of my child, not much because he's saving for a holiday with his mates. I'd love to go but there's no way he'll take me and his son. I certainly need a holiday. Perhaps he'll find someone else on his holidays; it wouldn't be the first time, he's done it twice before, but I love him too much to lose him, and with a baby I wouldn't be able to find someone else very easily. I'll hold on to him as long as I can; if our relationship was up to him we would have finished while I was expecting our son.

But in a way, I'll never lose my boyfriend as I have his baby to love.

You're only young once. Make the most of it.

SCHOOL DAYS ◄

SANJIT KAUR BAGRY

Telford, Shropshire

My name is Sanjit and I live in Telford with my mum and dad and three brothers. We own two shops, but only one is running and we also own a house. We used to live in Wolverhampton but moved to Telford in 1981.

When my dad told us that we were moving, I thought great, what a nice break it will be from Wolverhampton. But when we moved to Telford I found it was different from what I thought it would be.

We first bought a corner shop in Madeley and the house was in Woodside. I thought the house was very nice but no other Asian family lived around us. I was eleven and didn't know much about racism but I did know a bit about the National Front. The first day when we were about to move in, we had a note through the door saying something like 'We don't need you here black bastards'. The letters NF were written on the front of our door. Even though I didn't know much about them, I did know that we were going to get some trouble around here. My mum was a little worried but my dad said it would soon pass.

When we settled down, me and my brother decided to play outside. While we were playing on our bikes a boy about ten came over and started to make trouble by calling me names such as Paki, saying niggers aren't welcome here. We started making friends around the neighbourhood after two or three months, but there was still this little prat and his mates who kept going on and on. We tried hard to ignore them but it was hard, so we'd get into fights and we would get the blame.

I think the worst experience came at school, because I was on my own, without my brothers to stick up for me.

I was taken to my tutor group by the headmaster. I walked into the class behind him and I could feel pairs of eyes looking at me as though a leper had walked in. The headmaster introduced me to the tutor who seemed like a nice man. As soon as the headmaster left I could hear whispering behind me. I heard lots of things I had heard in my neighbourhood, but something really hit me. 'They should go back to their own country.' I was in my own country, I was born here. This is what they didn't know and I knew I was not welcome. A girl took me around the school.

My first lesson was music. I really like music except I knew I wasn't going to like this lesson. Two boys sitting opposite me kept laughing. I couldn't figure out what was so funny until a girl told them to stop taking the piss. They were making fun of me.

In maths we had a test and I finished first and got the top mark. 'Blackie is brainy,' I heard.

It took me a couple of months to make friends with some of the girls. I hadn't made friends with any of the boys because I found they were the more racist, though there was the odd girl too.

One day in home economics lesson, a boy was making so many racist remarks that he really got on my nerves. I told him to shut up or else. He didn't shut up because he was in front of all his friends, so I went over to him and pushed him. He thumped me so I got hold of him and swung him around. He landed on a table with his arm twisted. He shut up after that.

I don't know what it was, but from that day on I started making more friends with the boys and started getting less racial abuse. I guess I had to show them that they couldn't push me around any more.

In the fourth and fifth year I got to know more people. In

the fifth year I found that I got on with the boys a bit more than the girls because I am into doing boys' stuff such as wearing ties, shirts and other boys' things. At the end of the fifth year I even played cricket with the boys, so you can see how it changed gradually over the years.

The latest remark I got at the end of the fifth year was: 'We got used to her'. I don't think this boy meant it in a racist way because we are really good friends.

But this made me think. Why did they have to get used to me? I was like everyone else. Why was it me they had to get used to? I don't think anyone should go through this kind of experience because it is very upsetting at times.

After this experience, I was afraid of going to college this year in case I had to go through the same experience again. But I found it was very different. I made friends quite quickly.

Even though I get odd remarks from my friends I don't take them so seriously because I know that they are only joking. But if I get a remark from someone I don't know, well, I just ignore them or tell them to grow up. But most of the time my friends stick up for me so I don't have to say anything for myself.

MARGARET ADDISON

South Petherton, Somerset

Taking exams must be one of the most frightening and nervous experiences that anyone must endure through the period of being a teenager. It is not so much the actual taking of the exams themselves which is so awful, although of course they contribute a great deal to the general feeling of fear; no, the most awful time comes at the beginning and at the end.

The beginning is the time when you are meant to revise. Revision is a terrible time – both if you revise and if you don't. Firstly, if you revise, poring over a file brimming with A4 pages covered in your untidy handwriting, you suddenly wish not only had you written everything down a bit clearer, but also that you had started revision a damn sight earlier. However, once resigned to the fact that you can't put the clock back, you prepare to dedicate yourself to full and thorough revision, discarding all else in life. It sounds impressive when you first tell yourself that this is what you intend to do; no more coming home at two o'clock in the morning after a night on the town, no more watching endless soap operas and quiz shows on the television just because you couldn't think of anything better to do (or couldn't be bothered to get out of your comfortable position in the armchair to switch off the television set). No, somehow you are going to forget that life exists outside revision. Of course such a harsh decision is absolutely impossible to carry out, although you do try to kid yourself at the time that you can undertake it easily – all it needs is a little willpower and of course you have got lots of that!

Even knowing subconsciously that what you have re-solved to do will be virtually impossible, you are surprised when you are tempted by more enjoyable activities which interest you more than the coal-mining industry and iron and steel in the seventeenth century. The fact is, you hadn't realised how *boring* revision could be! Of course you have been advised by various lecturers on a number of exam techniques, favouring 'active' rather than 'passive' revision. You almost end up believing that you are meant to find revision an enjoyable pastime, recalling all the many happy lessons you have experienced. But the hard truth is revision *is* boring, unless you are incredibly interested in the subject; it can even cause the dedicated student to fall asleep over the pages informing him of the factors that caused the Industrial Revolution to take place when it did.

Perhaps one of the most important reasons for this boredom is that you didn't fully realise how much material you had to cover in such a short space of time. Therefore you become easily distracted, finding you have a sudden and irrepressible urge to tidy up your room, even though it has looked like a pigsty for the last three months, and the only time you normally clean it up is when your mother keeps nagging at you (about fifty times before you usually respond!) or when Aunt Amanda has come down to stay, and she is to sleep in your room, so you feel obliged to make a bit of an effort in the art of housework. When you are tempted away from your studying by such strange diversions, you are trespassing on the territory of the second category concerning revision – namely those who choose not to revise. Now, that category itself is split into two sections – those who do not revise because they are not particularly concerned about their performance in the forthcoming exam, and the second section (which is far more common), namely those who know they need and should get down to hard studying, but somehow have neither got the determination or willpower to force themselves to sit down for hours on end digesting the wonders of pure mathematics.

Now, this particular section of the second category (in which we have all from time to time found ourselves) suffer the most severe guilt complexes over their lack of revision. Although they are aware that they should be studying they cannot somehow bring themselves to the dreaded task; temptation has won over what they know they should be doing, and in a way they suffer far more than those who eventually find the willpower and determination to sit down and revise. For, whilst the second category are appearing to be carefree and enjoying the pleasures life has thrown in their way, a nagging little voice at the back of their minds is preventing them from totally enjoying themselves, reminding them that the economics exam is only in eight days' time and hadn't they better sit down and do some revision before it is too late? Otherwise they might have a complete shock when they get into the exam, look at the paper and suddenly realise that they haven't got a hope in hell of answering the questions, or worse still, that their mind will go completely blank. They will not even be able to resort to the technique known as 'waffle'.

So revision, therefore, is the beginning part of examinations which is in some ways worse than the exams themselves. But outside the hall everyone panics, clutching their pencil cases, candidate numbers and gripping tubes of Polos and glucose tablets in their sweaty fists. The absurd hope is that the sweets, especially the latter items, are going to give them extra energy in the exam, and calm their nerves in such a way that they are going to produce the best essays they have ever written in their lives. It is true, then, that you yourself will begin to find yourself slipping into the realms of 'pre-exam panic mania'!

However, it can be argued that you are merely in a situation of extended revision period, for the taking of exams does not actually begin until you find yourself sitting in the hall surrounded by other fellow students, about to look for the first time at the question paper. This theory of waiting outside the hall for the exam as a continuation of revision time is further strengthened by the fact that you are bound to see a handful of students clutching revision cards, their eyes popping out of their heads in a vain attempt to remember all those important history dates five minutes before they are due to sit the actual exam.

'Pre-exam panic mania' has got you securely in its grip, and you find yourself seriously doubting, perhaps for the first time, whether you really do know those facts you took so long (and you thought thoroughly) to revise. Indeed, you end up walking over to one of those last-minute revisers, just to check on a few details that you already know. Then, suddenly, the great doors open, and a figure (usually looking very official and serious) emerges, a great list in hand, on which is written the name of each individual candidate. Silence falls amongst the throng of nervous students, an unnatural silence. This is it! This is where all the revision is to display itself visually in an attempt to impress the examiner. All this worry and stress just for an exam that will last at most a few hours. Surely this is just lunacy? But it is either going to make or break your academic career.

Once in the hall, seated at your little desk which you find is one of the only wobbly ones in the room (so that every time you write something down it looks as if you were writing on the deck of a Sealink ferry experiencing a bad crossing), you are suddenly alarmed by the large amount of pure white A4 lined and margined paper. This makes you seriously wonder whether you know enough about anything (let alone the subject you are being examined on) to fill up all those sides of file paper.

If all else fails, you at least know that you have only got to endure the situation for a few hours at the most before you are released. If you are feeling particularly brave, you could leave the hall on your own accord after the first hour, although be prepared to have the whole hall of students take their eyes off their work for a moment to scrutinise you, smirking to themselves, knowing that at least one other person is going to do worse than they themselves.

The most annoying sounds in the hall, if you stay, are the noises of paper being noisily and hurriedly torn as students cram endless numbers of sweets into their mouths, producing the famous noise of the boiled-sweet being sucked, or the crunch as some over-enthusiastic student brings the molars down on a poor, unfortunate Polo. You hear the invigilator's squeaky shoe as he brings more file paper either to a terribly brainy student who has written a page even before anyone else has even looked at the questions, or else to someone who has made such a mess of his paper that he has decided to start again.

The inquests of the exam paper at the end are something which you would do better to avoid if possible. Even if you have come out of the hall feeling reasonably confident, the student inquest will make you leave feeling you have answered every question wrongly and have completely failed.

The end of the exam procedure, which is in some cases worse than the revision period, and the actual taking of the exams, is awaiting the results. This is made worse by the fact that you have to wait about two months for them. Perhaps this is why people go on holiday or get a summer job just to take their minds off the subject.

Whilst waiting you can't do much about your old school work. You feel that it is very hard to resist the temptation to have a ritual bonfire, with all your folders of notes in place of the logs, but at the same time you feel that you had better keep all your notes intact in case you discover you have failed and need to re-take all your subjects.

The climax is the day when you know that the postman is to deliver the letter (always in a brown envelope to make it look more official and frightening) which will inform you how badly (or how well, if you are lucky!) you have done. That day you get up very early and sit by the window overlooking the front of the house so you will be the first member of your family to see him come cycling along on an old red bicycle.

The fact that you are sitting by the window about two hours before the postman is due to arrive is beside the point. The only thing you are conscious of is that you must be the first to get the post (so if you have failed you can run upstairs and lock yourself in the bathroom to cry your eyes out in private). When the postman does appear, your heart is thumping so much that you think you might fall down the stairs. You run out of the house informing your family (and the world) that *you will get the post this morning*. The postman gives you a look of surprise (unless he has already encountered other desperate students) when you stick out a trembling hand and grab the post, ignoring his cheery comment on how nice the weather is today.

The envelope is to inform you whether the academic world (and also society in general) considers you a failure or a success, whether you can get the job you wanted, or go to the university or polytechnic you wished to attend. That envelope is to contain the key to your future and, perhaps most importantly of all, to inform you whether you need to suffer again the horrors of exams.

CATHERINE HISCOCK

Maidstone, Kent

You must know the feeling. You're sitting in your bedroom trying to study, impossibly trying to cram three topics in the night before the exam, when your favourite song comes on the radio, or worst of all, the sun comes out.

That's it, that really does it. The urge to revise has well and truly died on the doorstep. Perhaps it never came through the door in the first instance. It might have done in the lower sixth, when you're smug with your shining new intellectual self, eager to impress the tutors and dreaming deludingly of post-graduate research after a shining university career. I'm afraid the sun gets to you in the end, and you gladly submit your pale self to it.

The image described above, that of the new sixth year, disintegrates anyway, by the eve of the upper sixth. You lost it in drinking contests, all-night parties, rattling round Italian campsites in a decrepit Catholic minibus with the former hippy who taught you English literature, working in pubs where you learn to smile tolerantly at insults and invitations, 'watching 'The Young Ones' and the parents' divorces.

You develop a devil-may-care attitude to life, and most of all to *work*. Saying this word to an upper sixth who appears to have a permanent hangover is like showing a crucifix to a vampire, or even showing the strait-laced Head of the Sixth Form to someone who turns up the stereo extremely loud and starts engaging in a personal relationship behind the drinks machine.

So that, now, as you sit here not revising, you know you'll be lucky to manage a course at a polytechnic. Passing these 'A' levels with good grades will entitle you to freedom

44

for possibly the first time, even though university is like a mirage, a dream you were lucky to have once. But at the moment, I know I'd much rather read a good novel, sunbathe in what little Britain gets of the sun, get creative, inspired and write poetry, have a wild month on a mountain and lead an unadulterated hedonistic lifestyle. Wouldn't that be fantastic? The trouble is, I've done nothing to deserve it: I haven't worked.

'A' level courses don't encourage creativity. Perhaps that's why I'm not writing poetry or doing revision. You're constantly living in the shadows of Dylan Thomas, T.S. Eliot *et al* on an English lit. course. You're so impressed you want to emulate them, or in the essays you have to regurgitate their points of view or the tutor's received opinions, because at the end of the day that's what the examiner wants to read: that you understand what 'Poem in October' means.

Besides, in practice, you're not allowed to be creative at eighteen years old. You've just become an adult (what the hell's that?), and you're expected to get ahead with practical matters such as careers and families, not vegetate over cosmic principles or rhyming couplets. That comes later, after what every 'good' poet or novelist must have had: 'experience'. What a deeply talismanic word. I can imagine old people wearing stones round their necks engraved with that word.

Let's forget youthful poetic aspirations. They don't make the world go round. You've just finished having other people's creativity rammed down your throat for seven years and are masochistically about to do it again for another three years, of your own free will, feeling like a parasite on your father's wallet, and unlikely to have a high-flying job to pay him back with.

This outburst of pen on paper is probably due to what

45

must be academia's equivalent of post-natal depression. The main problem is that you haven't given birth to a perfect baby who will have a stable future, but to some rather weak exam papers full of poor structure or complete error which, unless the examiner is non-intelligent, mad, or both, will not guarantee you entry to university, never mind a future.

Yet Hope's light still flickers in the long months before the results come out, and you begin to dream, 'Just suppose I did pass . . .' Then a manic depressive moodswing descends and you sit in Hamlet-like thought, meditating on everything from 'God, if I don't get an A in maths/English/biology, I'm going to walk under a juggernaut' to 'I've just decided that further education is going to be a complete and utter waste of time, and I never want to look at a physics/French/art/history textbook ever again'.

So you go out and look for a job, quite optimistically, because you've got millions of 'O' levels. Your name goes down on every file in town, you go to the Job Centre so often that it becomes a second home – and still no job. Your parents accept the fact that employers don't want temporary workers who could be leaving them in the lurch in October, and yet they still make it so clear they don't want an unemployed eighteen-year-old around that you consider joining the hippy peace convoy, rejecting society, parental rule, the 'system', and all creature comforts in favour of discovering your real self, eating burnt sausages and living in a bus with twenty other rather smelly people.

Of course, parents don't seem to understand that doing absolutely nothing is an enriching experience, and continually remind you that at your age they were out working for a living, and don't see why you shouldn't support yourself partially or totally at university, a place they view as a pot-smoking hippy dosshouse where the worst species

46

of the younger generation congregate to listen to doddery lecturers who haven't the faintest idea which century it is, to get drunk seven nights a week, to start a prolific and somewhat dubious sex life, to squander grants, and to give up anything distantly related to work. They have no idea these things are contributory factors to the makings of great poets and novelists.

But what's the use of being creative, they cry, when a Master of Arts, in a country where unemployment is so high, is likely to be found in the dole queue or amongst three hundred applicants for a job as a milkman?

They're quite right, unfortunately, and leave you re-thinking your motives and stewing in self-doubt once more, not getting your revision done, and perhaps, in the long run, not going to university.

And that won't be too surprising, when the only things you have to show for a summer of revision and exams are an enviable tan, a capacity for large amounts of alcohol, and a fully detailed knowledge of the witty repartee between Dirty Den and Angie, Sheila Grant and Matty, and just about every sick-making detail from 'Sons and Daughters'.

The entire population of eighteen-year-old, ex-sixth formers in Britain await August with razor blades, whisky, pickaxes, smelling salts and the overpowering charm of the professional crawler. There is nothing suicidal about them, despite all appearances. In fact, they are prepared to blackmail their referees into pleading with admissions tutors in view of bad grades: 'Look, Mr . . . I know he/she did quite awfully in the exam, but I can assure you he/she has produced some excellent work during the last two years, some of which I might possibly send you . . . Yes, he/she is here now, and quite upset to have done so badly . . .'

You and I will only have ourselves to blame.

London

This was it, the end of a perfect holiday and I had to go back and read my future which would arrive in two white envelopes.

I knew my parents wanted me to do well, and I knew that some of my teachers expected that I wouldn't, so for those two reasons I wanted to do well. But for myself, I didn't really seem to be bothered by it all very much, which surprised me. My mum did all my worrying for me, and I don't know who did most of my revising – but I know I didn't do as much as I should have done!

On the day of our departure from Spain I woke up early and my first thoughts were of my results which were at home waiting for me. What a welcome home! I wasn't quite sure whether to expect bad results or good results, so I expected bad. That way I couldn't be disappointed!

I packed quickly, as if that would get me home to those two envelopes faster. I was so curious. To my surprise I wasn't nervous and I didn't have butterflies. At the airport waiting for the plane, I forgot about it all for a while. In the taxi home I thought about the holiday and about how I'd forced the thought of results out of my head since I'd taken the exams. I went over the plans I'd made weeks before. I'd get home, rush in, run up the stairs, get the envelopes, go to my room, shut myself in, and read the results.

We got home. I rushed upstairs, grabbed all my mail, went to my room and shut the door. I sat on my bed and stared at my pile of mail, trying to figure out whether or not I was nervous, excited or suicidal! I couldn't decide on any of them, so I decided to go through the pile of mail as I picked it up. On top was a postcard from a friend, so I read that. But I didn't really take in what was on the card.

Suddenly, I was in a real hurry, so I tore open the envelope. So much so that it ended up practically in shreds! Out of the envelope came a pathetic slip of thin paper and a note from the school. I was shocked to see that my hands were shaking slightly when I picked up the slip.

Five 'O' levels and one CSE.

I stayed sitting on my bed for a while just letting the results sink in. I was pleased with my marks, except biology because it was the subject I'd revised most for and I got a U! I wanted to tell my family and my friends quickly. I also wanted to compare marks with my school friends. But I didn't phone them in case they'd not done well and I didn't want to sound big-headed. So I went slowly downstairs to tell my mum. She asked me what I'd got and I said 'Well . . . they're not very good,' and tried to look doubtful as if I'd failed them all.

I read her the results starting with the U and going upwards. She gave a big yell and hugged me. I guessed she was pleased! I then rang my dad who was over the moon. And I phoned some friends, but not school friends. I'd wait until I saw them to find out what they'd got.

Then we celebrated and a couple of people came over. Of course, the best bit of passing exams is the champagne people buy you!

At school I found out that all my mates had failed. They didn't seem to mind but it did make me wonder what I'd be doing if I'd failed. I had expected to, and didn't like the idea of re-taking 'O' levels. So I had thought about leaving school.

My friends have started a CPVE course while I have started 'A' levels. It was odd at first not having my mates around all the time to talk to and gossip with. It was also boring, so much so that I thought of giving up 'A' levels. But I kept going because everyone makes so much of the exams you have and, for what I think I want to do later, I need certain qualifications. So I decided to stay on and make the most of it.

One day I'll probably be glad.

CATHERINE BULL

Littleover, Derby

Slowly, I looked behind me. I remembered how scared I was and how small I had felt the first time I walked through those school gates. Now it was all over it felt like an anti-climax. What was going to happen next? Where do we all go next? We all seemed to be asking the same questions. I remembered the good times, how many friends I had made, the laughs we had all had together, the school trips and parties. As I walk out of those gates I don't feel like laughing. I wonder what all my old friends will look like in twenty years' time. How many of the girls I knew who had high hopes and aspirations would end up unmarried mothers or drug addicts? I bet my gran didn't walk out of school wondering how many of her friends would be drug addicts. The unsheltered world outside those school gates seemed even worse than when I entered the school building at the beginning of my school career. My life has already been mapped out for the next two and a half years. I want to do the course but I am very apprehensive about it. I don't really know what to expect. I can't help wondering if all the hard work, all the revising and sitting stressful exams is all going to be worth it. There are so many people

50

who are unemployed and not all of them have no qualifications. I hope that whatever else happens, I never have to turn to the dole queue.

Now that I have left school, I begin to realise how many friends I will lose, but then again I must try to think of the new friends I will find at college. I must learn to start growing up. I am sixteen and still treated like a child by the government and the laws of this country but in society I have pressure put on me to be an adult. As I walk towards the graffiti-covered school gates, I see my name scrawled onto the brickwork. I had left my mark but now it was time to face and turn to the outside world.

Another thought that goes through my mind is, did my parents really go through the same pressures or did they have an easier time? Surely not, they could walk into any job they liked when they left school. Somewhere, someone has done something wrong and now, we, the young people, are having to pay the price. I hope that by the time I have children, the government will have sorted out the country and that my children will not have any problems in finding jobs and they will have a brighter future.

My younger sister has just started secondary school. With some luck, her life after she leaves school will be more promising. With the introduction of the new exams, things might change. I hope she doesn't feel the same way as I feel about our country when she walks out of those big school gates.

SAM JONES

Upper Basildon, Berkshire

My story starts on 16 December 1981. It's a funny thing to write about, but it's the only thing that has dramatically changed my life. I was sitting at the table happily eating my cornflakes when I fell off my chair. There I lay on the floor unconscious for no apparent reason. My grandma fetched my mother who promptly took me to hospital. I was unconscious for six days and when I regained my consciousness I started having fits much like epileptic fits. I was tested for brain tumours and damage to the skull but nothing was apparent.

I had these fits every two to three minutes during which I was unconscious but my mum said that as soon as I'd stopped having a fit it seemed as if I proceeded to have another one. She explains them to me like so:

Sam would twitch a lot on her left-hand side only. She would lose complete control of herself and sometimes wet herself; she would stare until her lips turned blue, and shake, and swallow her tongue, which could be very dangerous.

I was in hospital over Christmas and the New Year which was miserable for my family. My father and my brother had to cope on their own; my mother stayed with me because at one stage it was thought that I would die.

Eventually the doctors came up with the fact that I had got encephalitis which caused the brain damage and left me with temporal lobe epilepsy. They said it was a germ in the air that one in a billion people could catch and I just happened to catch it.

The damage to my brain naturally affected my school work. I had forgotten everything, even who my mum was at one stage. Therefore I had to learn to spell, do my tables, everything all over again. This meant being absent from school for about six months. Of course I wasn't as clever anymore anyway, because the damage was quite severe. Before, I was quite bright, not outstanding, but I was in the top groups for all lessons. I am now in the middle and although my parents tell me I'm clever, I still feel like a failure towards them and to myself.

When I was in hospital I was at a state school who were lovely to me. I got a separate card from everyone in the school, even the toddlers. We then moved to Warwickshire with my father's job. All was well there, I had fits only about every month but then I started having small turns, in the family known as funny turns; in my mind weird things were happening which I can't even describe to the doctors. All I can say is that I feel like Alice when she was falling down the hole in *Alice in Wonderland*. I am in another world; frightening things happen. I had these turns up to three times a day; they lasted no more than three minutes and when they were over, I was fine.

I then grew too old for that school. I took my Common Entrance and as my dad moved around so much, I was sent to boarding school at Westonbirt. It was great fun, I had a wonderful time; the games were lacrosse and netball in the winter and tennis, swimming and rounders in the summer. The academic standard was quite high but it suited me just fine. If I had a fit or funny turn all they did was increase the dose. At one stage I was on fifteen pills a day.

When I started my periods my fits got worse and worse. When I did games I was liable to have a fit, therefore I was off games for the term which depressed me, as I loved games dearly. All I seemed to do was get depressed over small things that people said like, 'she'll have an eppi on me' or, 'she's got brain damage'. Being epileptic, I had to be quite tough, but these remarks hit me deep down and I was often hurt.

My fits are still getting worse. Last term being a nine-week term was short, but it was very short for me as I was there for only three weeks. For the rest of the time I was either in the sanatorium, at home or in hospital. The doctors do tests such as brain-scans and EEGs, but no proof of a tumour is ever found, just severe damage.

I have not yet said why the fits happen. They come when I get hot, for example, I once had one in the bath. My mum was on the telephone, therefore I nearly drowned. I now have to sing in the bath (my poor family!). Also during games I get hot, which explains the reason why I was off games.

About ten months ago I had a very, very severe fit where the whole left-hand side of my body was affected. My left foot turns in badly when I walk now and since then I have had a terrible headache. Yes, for ten months! It's hard; I have to act as if it's not there, otherwise I'd have no friends. You know what it's like, 'Oh she's in a mood again.' All because of a headache. I try not to show that my head is hurting during the day; when I say 'My head's killing me', people tend to think of me as a hypochondriac, which is yet another thing I find hard to accept. Nobody seems to understand, so I talk to my matron, a young girl of twenty-five.

Anyway, my funny turns turned into mini-fits, known to us as attacks because they are worse. I shake just like in a fit; the only thing is I'm still conscious. I then found Mo, a girl in the year above who gets bad asthma. This was someone that fully understood, wouldn't laugh and talk behind my back. I could *trust* her. We talk together and are now very close.

Unfortunately, I now have to leave Westonbirt due to

54

my fits. Really the solution is not to do games but when I see everyone playing I feel so left out and though there are many people in the world much worse off than I am, I still haven't learnt to face the facts. Also deep down I need to be with my parents, as when I'm in the san the only thing I think about in my lonesome bed is my mum and dad.

This is about the end of my story about epilepsy; many other things have happened, but this incident affected me the most. If there are others like me, don't worry. Try not to get down, chin up and maybe your problem will be solved. I haven't said so far but the one thing, the only thing, in the world I want to be is a famous actress and singer, and though many people have said to me that epilepsy is a great disadvantage, I'm going to make it. When you see me on the silver screen, I hope this will encourage others like me.

STARTING ◄
UNIVERSITY

AMANDA SMITH

Oadby, Leicestershire

The train rattles on, slicing like a knife through the darkness. The fields are slipping past, miles of empty track away behind me. All this ground I have cleared since the morning. All this ground since home . . . since leaving them.

I lean my forehead against the window. It feels cold on my skin, like ice. I think that I might cry. I can feel the force of a few angry tears welling up in my throat, but I will not let them push through into the open. In my mind they are like evil little tongues, wagging maliciously, aching to tell the whole world of my weakness.

I am thinking of the old life that I woke up to this morning, seeing nothing beyond the summer, not really believing, not even at the last moment, that it could ever end. Tonight I will go to bed and already my new life will have started – university, fending for myself, all that freedom to drown in . . . I try in my mind to recall the images of the morning, those last moments, and for a split second I seem to picture them: my parents sitting on a platform bench, staring down at the concrete ground, as a plastic cup scuttles in the wind and plunges into the pit where the rails are sleeping. This morning, as we sat waiting for the train, my thoughts froze. An automatic act of self-preservation. If you become maudlin, they stall your mind. At times it was good advice for me, but advice can't help me now . . . my mind is a mess. I begin to cry.

'Kiss me!' The drunkard in the opposite seat smiles suddenly. I sit up, startled by his latest advance. Has he seen my tears, I wonder.

'Kismet!' he repeats. This time his speech is clearer to

59

me. 'It means fate,' he explains. 'Kismet, Hardy!'

I have no idea what he is babbling on about. He has been pestering me intermittently ever since he got on the train at York. Mostly he sleeps, but now and then he wakes up to take swigs from the two bottles that he keeps in the inside pockets of his jacket. One contains whisky, the other coke. Fortunately, for now, he seems to have called a halt to any great monologue that he might have planned, and I breathe a sigh of relief.

But no. 'Did you happen to know,' he begins, 'that I am an artist?'

'No,' I reply bluntly.

'Come here!' he says. 'I'll do a portrait of your lovely face.'

I feel slightly alarmed at this declaration. He pulls out a pen and a child's drawing pad from the plastic Tesco's bag by his side. Then, with the tip of his tongue firmly fixed between his brown teeth, and his eyebrows knitted solidly together, he begins to sketch my face. His movements are hasty and brisk as if he knows what he is doing. It is obvious to me that he does not. But as for himself, he seems convinced by his own charade.

'There!' he exclaims triumphantly, as he slides the pad across the table. I gaze down at a mass of unsteady lines. Somewhere I can pick out a childish attempt at an eye. I smile at him. Inside I am disgusted.

'See my name,' he breathes, pointing to a scrawl at the foot of the page. 'The Lightning Flash – that's me.' He touches his chest, dislodging one or two crumbs from his pullover.

'Take it,' he smiles. 'And you must, of course . . .' he leans forward, waving his index finger in the air for emphasis, '. . . come to my party!' He takes back the page and begins to write on the reverse side.

'Next Saturday. You come. Thirteen – Prince's – Street – Aberdeen.' He pronounces each word as he writes it, slowly and laboriously. 'We will have cakes.' He writes 'cakes' beneath the address and then proceeds with his list – 'crisps – lemonade – sandwiches – a little booze'. He scrawls what looks like 'drink' at the bottom of the list, then comes to an abrupt halt.

I take the page, smile gratefully, and put it away with a show of extreme care.

'I'll throw it away,' I think now. 'As soon as I find a bin.' I have a bad feeling about it now, as if this slip of paper, neatly tucked away in my handbag, is some sort of omen of doom. The drunkard is fast asleep at this moment. He is snoozing peacefully.

'Fate,' I think with cynicism. 'You've given yourself over to it, you stupid old man . . . and just look what has happened. Don't you know you have to fight for what you want? It doesn't just simply arrive. You have to fight, and you have to live. Why can't you be like that American girl? She lives . . . doesn't she just! Why should I waste my thoughts on this old failure,' I ask myself, and I resolve to think of the American girl.

It was at Derby that I had to wait three-quarters of an hour for my connection. I dragged all my cases over to the platform, seated myself on a bench and pulled out my packed lunch . . . cheese and tomato sandwiches, an apple and a bar of chocolate. It was there that I met her.

'I'm doing Europe,' she drawled. 'Travelling for one year. I'm doing the States also.'

'You're alone?' I enquired.

'Sure I am! My God! It's the only way to do it!'

'But it's dangerous.'

'That's the thrill!'

The American girl was sure of herself in every respect, in

61

the way she spoke, wheeled her bicycle along the platform, even in the way she threw biscuits at scavenging pigeons.

'Wouldn't it be great to be like that?' I whispered to myself later as I stood rocking to and fro on the soggy floor of the train toilet, gazing into the filthy mirror, trying to find a glimmer in my dull eyes. I wondered where she found her strength. I always seemed to lack a place inside me where strength could find an anchorage.

'I wish I was Irish, or something,' I thought. 'I wish I had green eyes.' But they weren't green, they were dull. They didn't reflect any hazy moorlands, any villages steeped in tradition and mystery. There was nothing to hold me down, no pride, no sense of belonging.

I even began to wish that I'd come from the slums. Slums had songs written about them . . . dirt turned to glamour. Where I came from was caught in a space between the gloss and the filth, the middle of the road space where no one ever comes for inspiration.

'But it is my home,' I think now, and for once it begins to seem vaguely substantial, set against that strange, shell-like world outside.

Is that Edinburgh creeping up on me now? Groups of orange and yellow lights . . . here and there the white glow of a living room . . . brighter and brighter those lights . . . just as I think I'm about to find some scrap of comfort in my mind, they come and blind me.

Over the intercom, the guard announces Waverly Station. A scruffy-looking youth at the far end of the carriage pulls back his headphones and seems to sigh. Quickly he pulls together his luggage and disappears into the doorway section, jolting in time with the train. The automatic door stutters to a close while the train slows in fits and starts.

The Lightning Flash stirs, unwraps a mint and slips it between his thin lips. He nauseates me. 'Why don't you get off?' I enquire silently. He knows all about me, I think suddenly. He knows of my weakness. Damn! I shouldn't have let it slip. I'm old enough . . .

From the blackness we roll into the warmth of Waverly Station. Brightness, movement . . . it looks like heat, but as we roll to a halt I can see the cold.

A man waits in expectation, stands poised in the centre of the mass of passengers newly arrived at Edinburgh. He stands still in all the confusion, his feet rooted to the scarred, grey concrete. In his right hand is a cigarette which he holds queerly, inwards. His left hand is thrust into his pocket for warmth. His face is grained like granite. Breath is clouding out in front of his eyes, eyes that look like a sparrow's. He is waiting for a wife, I think, a daughter . . . a friend.

The crowd drifts on, people get on and off . . . some smile, not many. Most tighten themselves body and soul against the cold and the dark. A scrap of newspaper entangles itself around the feet of the waiting man. He ignores it. He ignores everything.

Hardened. Why are they all hardened, when I feel so vulnerable? Time will make me like them. It will make or break me. I will cope or I will crumble and fold up like the drunkard, a child forever.

The train is moving, pulling out. Suddenly I realise that the waiting man is out of view. I will never know if his rendezvous took place. What sort of a person could make him smile? I'll never know.

I hate this journey. I wish that it were over. I can't stand all these faces, all carrying their own lives, guarding them viciously. I'm upset, I know. Disorientated. Confused. There is a rumble below, and the drunkard turns his vague, stupid head to me.

'This is the Forth Bridge,' he wheezes, tapping the

window with his stained fingers. 'Look.'

I watch the shadows outside and feel the ground leave us; suddenly we are suspended over water. The wheels of the train are beating time over the track, the same rhythm, only now with a just-perceptible hollowness. I ignore the drunkard and stare out at the small, unsteady lights that must be boats on the water. Out of the darkness, between the flickering lights of the opposite shores, my own face wavers like a ghost. It is young and tired, staring back at me from my own reflection in the glass.

Today, I think, I have not felt young and I have not felt old. I am travelling between the two, caught in transition. Always extremes are in my mind . . . youth, old age, success, failure . . . always extremes. Why can't I accept the here and now? Why must I always be yearning for the past, or thinking of the future? Always the beginning or the end of it all. I hate this time, the growing and maturing, never feeling the same for two moments in succession. I hate the changes and the pain they cause. Life seems to be nothing but an endless confusion, foundering in hope, fear . . . incomplete knowledge. One day it has to come together. One day.

Leuchars in an hour. And then university begins . . . a new life. I am terrified. Speeding through the dark, that is all I seem to know. I would exchange all their pride for disappointment, just to be back there in the warmth without this god-awful train, this blackness . . . and, between me and the water, that gaping fall below.

London

Going away to London, or rather to university was something that I had been waiting for for years.

As a first generation Sikh girl living in Britain the influences upon my life have been very different from those which have shaped the attitudes of my parents and never were the differences between us more pronounced than through my mid-teens.

My parents had always been very proud of my academic achievements. Education is always looked upon with esteem by the 'community' and therefore my getting to university only heightened this feeling of success for them. For me, university meant a chance to be free of the restrictions an Asian girl is always under and keeping my parents content at the same time.

The one thing that marred their pleasure at one of their offspring achieving a place at university was that fact that I was a girl. I come from a family of three girls and one boy, it was always expected that he would be the one to shine – to bring pride to the family. I remember vividly, the day before I left for London an aunt of mine asking my mother why it was me rather than my brother that was 'being allowed' to go to university.

Yet I had always known that if I could prove that I was capable of getting to university my parents (unlike some) would never have prevented me from doing so. That however did not mean that I went with their full enthusiasm.

Respectability is all important to an Asian family. Trying to keep the balance between staying 'respectable' and doing what I really wanted became more and more difficult from the sixth form on, when I really began to think for myself and question everything around me more than ever.

Why was it disrespectful to argue with my father if he was wrong? Why could I not be seen with boys around the town? What was wrong with going out to clubs and drinking? Asian parents seem to have very definite ideas about what constitutes respectability and even the slightest deviation can bring the whole wrath of the community to bear. An Indian girl who is seen not to respect her parents or their ideals is looked upon by the community as being 'bad'.

There is a comment, a rather bitter one perhaps, about how an Asian girl never leaves home unless it is with a husband or in a coffin; to some degree this does sadly contain an element of truth.

My going to London was a very difficult time for my parents. Maintaining the reputation of their daughters is all important to Asian parents. The shame of a 'fallen daughter' is insurmountable. Once her reputation has in any way been marred it reflects badly upon the whole family and ultimately it will hamper her parents' attempts to arrange a marriage with a respectable Indian boy. A daughter living away from home has her respectability under question. No longer under the auspices of either her parents or the watchful community, she is susceptible to all the 'evils' that she has so far in her life been shielded from. From my own experiences I feel that this realisation scares parents.

Their major fear is that their daughter will reject all they have tried to press upon her for a life which will bring shame on the family she leaves behind, and unhappiness for her. A 'badly' behaved daughter must come from a 'bad' family.

66

Living away from home and having the opportunity to discover various aspects of life that previously I was 'protected' from has made me realise more than ever just how subordinate to their men Indian women are. They seem to resign themselves to the fact that the men in the family will be able to dictate virtually every aspect of their lives without question. If university has taught me anything, it has been just that – to question – ruthlessly.

What perhaps I have seen to be the hardest thing of all about being an Asian girl living away from home is the choice that is to be made at the end of it all . . .

Any Asian girl in my position has had the opportunity for three or four years to discover life as it really is. Not the secure, protected, censored life of home, but a life where she can do whatever she pleases, whenever she pleases in an attempt to discover what *she* really wants and how she can get the life she wants for herself. What does she do next?

Does she reject the ideals her family hold to be 'right', does she decide that she can survive without the safety offered by the Asian society, the safety she has been used to? – or does she, as so many have done, return home and conform?

It is a hard choice to make, especially when you realise that rejecting the life your parents would want for you, a life they genuinely feel would make you happy, in effect, for most Asian girls, means rejecting your parents. A girl who refuses to conform, who openly defies her parents and the community, is a girl that any self-respecting parent would not allow to remain in their house. She has flaunted everything they stand for – she might possibly influence any other offspring to rebel as well, and therefore must be disowned.

The affection any child feels for someone who genuinely

cares and loves them and who is devoted to them is the crux of the problem. This affection and loyalty is in conflict with what you know is best for you.

For many, choosing to reject your past would mean never seeing your parents again and knowing that you are responsible for the torment and shame that they would go through.

The paradox of the whole situation and what angers me most, is that for an Asian son, his rejection of a traditional Asian life does not necessarily involve rejecting his parents. Perhaps one day this concession will include girls as well! It is a sad and confusing time for many of the Asian girls I have spoken to at university, especially for those who have realised that the one thing they can no longer accept or conform to is what symbolises the whole Asian culture – an arranged marriage.

Many for the first time will have had the opportunity to experience a real and full relationship. One that is full of warmth and love and friendship. To be suddenly expected to convey such affection to a person that you have not been able to 'discover' and get to like is often the deciding factor for many girls regarding the choice of life they make for themselves. It will probably be so for me.

What seems to be the greatest irony of the whole situation is how parents who love and care for their daughters, parents who strive harder and harder to try and make a comfortable and happy life for their girls can possibly look with horror or disapproval on the fact that their daughter has found happiness – by whatever means.

It is perhaps understandable that they find British life a threat to their culture, even to their religion, but the question that I often ask myself is: 'What is the point of either if it makes people unhappy?'

My parents' culture and religion has worked well for

them, but they never expected or wanted anything else. I know that I could have so much more and I am not prepared to give it up.

Any kind of education trains and encourages thought; so what is to happen as increasing numbers of Asian girls are allowed to go to university?

As this new band of independent, capable and confident young women grows, they will be able to give the help and guidance to one another that is lacking for girls like me today. That can only improve the status of Asian women, not only in the family and in the community, but in society in general, and that is something that is long overdue!

THE JOB — ◀
OR NO JOB

ANN-MARIE JEBBETT

Barwell, Leicestershire

I've felt a sense of urgency ever since I left school last month, scouring the job vacancy ads pinned to career noticeboards and in every daily newspaper. That urgency seems now to be substituted by fear.

I chewed anxiously on my fingernails. I glanced at my watch: 8.35 a.m. I withdrew a letter from a torn envelope which had been folded inside my handbag. I had re-read the letter so many times I could recall the words by heart.

It didn't contain the usual sympathy on the lines of: 'Your application as Office Junior has been unsuccessful, but we wish you success in finding a suitable position' etc . . . Just a chance of an interview glowed deep in my mind. I caught my reflection in the window of the bus. I stared back at the daunting face, covered in a mask of make-up as if trying to hide the identity of the person underneath it – ME. I rubbed the excess eyeshadow from my eyes and squinted a little at the window. I pressed my face against the cold glass, feeling its chill against my skin as the crowds of people scurried to and fro. They started to fade against the images forming in my mind as I drifted into a light sleep. My mind became unfocused on the images as I filtered through daydreams; I daydream a lot, too much according to my parents.

As the bus rolled down into the Leicestershire countryside, Madonna's raunchy effort, 'Like a Virgin', penetrated across the bus from a boy's Walkman. He was sitting opposite me. He looked up and smirked at me through the blond fringe that covered his left eye. I smiled back, not in recognition of him but of the presence of Madonna and her music. Though like many other girls I detested her image,

73

you really couldn't but feel a little proud of her originality of dress and her attitude towards life in general; her domination of the music scene in a still male-governed world proved that we women could make it to the top. But, of course, her looks, her figure and voice were her advantage, in comparison to my small, plump frame and appalling 'singing' vocals.

I picked up my magazine and flicked through the pages. The slender, tall models glazing the pages did nothing to ease my mind. But smiling red-headed Sarah Ferguson, whose curvy figure graced the back cover spontaneously brought a grin to my face as I reached for my Mars bar.

I had thought of nothing but my job interview since last Friday. It's a shock to think that I am now sixteen years old and will probably work until I'm twenty. I'll marry and by the time I'm thirty be blessed with two or three children, which will finalise our stereotyped family in Britain today. Not all women want that, do they? Maybe we don't have a choice, unless it means searching for that far-off dream. Yes, I know women are treated more independently now, but where I live, as soon as you leave school, girls are supposed to fit into a category of jobs: hosiery, clerical or hairdressing – though even those jobs are becoming few and far between now. Unemployment is still high in my area and there's still a lot of advice for school-leavers regarding their skills. But you can hardly answer your careers teacher: 'I want to be an author and a song writer.' They would probably look at me in complete amazement and push a careers leaflet into my hands either to do with college courses or starting up your own business! Even if I sent endless numbers of scripts to publishers, I would have to get a job to support me. It's unfair maybe, but perhaps it's a challenge to those who want to be successful in their own minds rather than those unwilling to make the effort.

74

I glanced back to the bus window. The hour I had spent perfecting my hairstyle now seemed like one minute; I watched in despair as my spikes started to waver, then fall gently to flatten themselves upon my head. I poked furiously at my hair, trying to achieve the impossible with its untamed waves. I wished now that I had brought my can of hairspray. I chuckled quietly to myself as I recalled the other uses my can of hairspray had found over the last few weeks. With my bedroom curtains closed, my bedside lamp as a spotlight and dressed in scanty clothing (clothes which I wouldn't dare wear in old, wary Barwell) and with either a can of hairspray or bottle of Impulse as a microphone, I could turn my bedroom into a stage from 'Top of the Pops' or 'The Tube'. I recalled imaginary interviews I had conducted on the edge of my bed, smiling and nodding my answers to questions posed by Jools Holland, Paula Yates or newspaper reporters and journalists from *Smash Hits* and *Just Seventeen*. Singing a duet in my bedroom mirror with Morten Harket from A-Ha to the twelve inch of 'Hunting High and Low' now seemed like a distant dream.

'Just practising becoming famous,' I would answer my mum, when she protested against my off-key singing which drowned out the sensual quality of Morten Harket's voice. Kissing A-Ha's poster, each member in turn, before I snuggled deep into my bed as I drifted into another dream. Maybe I thought, just maybe. It's not just the glamour and the money which attracts me to the career of songwriter and ever-hopeful singer. Being a household name enables you to do things which are impossible to do as an ordinary young girl.

Smoke hung in the air, causing me to cough. I turned round to watch a girl a little older than myself puff absentmindedly on a cigarette, its ash sparking red at the end as a sign of danger. As it dangled between two fingers of her right hand, I turned away in disgust. I felt her eyes glaring deep into my back; my spine tingled and shuddered in anticipation as she noticed my expression. I could hear her whistling to herself, her notes flowing against the noise of the bus engine. Oh yes, I had seen her type so many times, at my own school in fact. They would sit in groups on the walls outside the school gates, cross-legged in their school uniform, trying to look so sophisticated and adult.

I recalled back to last year when I read in our local newspaper that small, quiet Barwell, the village where I live, was in fact a central point for drugs dealing in the Midlands. Somehow Barwell villagers' attitudes changed towards the young people of the area. The media still continued to claim that fifteen- to sixteen-year-olds were at the most vulnerable age for smoking, drug-taking and that the number of teenage girls becoming pregnant was rising. Even as my friends and I walked along the streets of Barwell, you could feel the eyes of the villagers roaming your body from head to toe, trying to catch and notice the symptoms of addiction and pregnancy for local gossip.

I can't help but feel the sense of being watched in some shops, though. Shop assistants move closer towards you to watch your every move. It's ironic, but I was in Barwell's Co-op only last week and an elderly man was caught shoplifting. Tins of soup, packets of meat and biscuits were found hidden in the inside pockets of his overcoat. I couldn't help but allow a sarcastic smirk to light my face in triumph as he was questioned intently. I held my head high and walked out the shop with pride and my mum's shopping . . .

I felt a few raindrops wet upon my hand. Water was starting to form on my watch's face. Through its misty pane it read 9.05 a.m. The clouds were starting to disperse now, leaving the sky clearer as the bus entered Leicester. Just outside Leicester there is a tall white sign which features the words: 'You are now entering Leicester: a Nuclear Free Zone.' It stands proudly, half hidden by a nearby cluster of trees. After staring at it for a few minutes, I laughed quietly to myself. 'A Nuclear Free Zone,' I thought. Well that's a joke for a start, especially as there's a number of bombs directed for Leicester, Coventry and Birmingham – the three major cities of the Midlands; everyone within those cities would either be dead or badly injured. Though, after watching 'Threads' I was as frightened as everyone else; if there was a nuclear war, I thought, I would rather be killed outright instead of surviving in a lost world, or suffering from the fallout of radiation poisoning where you die a painful death. I recalled a quote that I once read, which had stuck in my mind ever since: 'Neither America nor Russia will start a Nuclear War, because neither knows what they're actually starting.'

The bus was now nearing my stop. My watch read 9.20 a.m. I gathered my bag and coat together and strolled with the other passengers towards the door. As I stepped out onto the pavement, I felt as hopeful and as panic-stricken as any other teenager, from whatever walk of life, facing their job interview . . . taking the next step up onto the next rung of the ladder of my life.

DONNA-MARIE McLOUGHLIN

Leeds, West Yorkshire

The eighties for me have been quite a memorable encounter. On 17 January 1980 I was twelve years old so I really wasn't a teenager to begin with. Looking back I feel that life has just flashed before me. I can remember as though it was yesterday. I don't suppose people realise the importance of each year that we approach. Each year is one step nearer to getting old. I don't suppose you realise how fast your life suddenly disappears into the past so quickly.

I think to myself that here I am, eighteen, working, and 1986 is soon on its way out. I realise how six years of the eighties have already gone by and another year approaches. How can somebody grow up so fast in six years and yet still remember these years as clear as day?

For me, the eighties were when I went to high school, did my exams, left school, got a job and I'm now working full time as a hairdresser. Not bad going in six years!

School is the first and last thing in your teenage years that you think about because without school, you're a nobody. I suppose you can say that part of your life is spent growing up in school, adjusting to the way of life, learning about life and how you go about it in the future.

The start of high school was pretty bad. I got a feeling of loneliness, it was a big school, and I had to make new friends. It was hard for me because I tend to be a bit shy when it comes to meeting new people. I always thought that people took a dislike to me, just because they looked at me in a funny way. Sort of paranoia, I suppose. I didn't really adjust to high school at all; maybe it was because I was rather an ambitious person. I'd always dreamed about being a hairdresser and one day running my own

78

salon, but it wasn't till I was about fourteen years old that I did seriously think about what I was going to do when I did eventually leave school.

I suppose I'd always been an outgoing person but never really showed it. I wanted to do things that I was sure would be right for me. I think though I developed a bit of a tearaway image. This was when my high school years began. I thought of myself as grown up the minute I stepped into that school. Unfortunately I began to lack confidence in myself. I developed a sort of barrier between me and my work at school. I began to think that I couldn't do this and I couldn't do that, always the one that got asked the question but never really had time to work the answer out because I was too busy talking. Maybe this is why I started to dress differently so I could hide behind this image that I'd created for myself. It didn't go down too well with the teacher at all. So the more I got told off the more I wanted to do it. I don't know why though.

I never used my ability. Probably it was laziness or maybe it was because I wasn't interested. With me, it seemed that all I had on my mind were ambitions. Hairdressing in particular. So obviously I didn't think that school was important. It was always me who was told to sit at the back of the class. Never any of my mates. (I'm not really blaming my mates because they weren't really distracting me.) It was probably the boredom of learning something that wasn't very interesting. So I suppose I did get carried away with talking.

When my final year did eventually come, then it was time to get down to some serious thinking. Thinking about exams and the future which was lying ahead. Even so I still didn't bother with my work. All that was interesting me was make-up, clothes and hair. Every day it was always the same, what should I wear to school today and how should I wear my hair? In the fifth form they were less strict about uniform rules, except that I was often told to get down to the toilets to wash that 'muck', which is what they used to call make-up, off my face. I used to dye my hair all different colours which is why they called me a walking advertisement for punks. I was trying to dress up for myself now and I did seem to get more attention. I suppose my ambitions were finally coming out on me.

Finally, I thought I could make something of my life on my own. That chance did come when I was offered a job in a hairdresser's after I left school. This was the hairdresser's that I was already working at on Saturdays. It was a job I'd been dreaming about all these years. I was so happy because it meant the first step to a good career. Unfortunately I had to do my exams before I started work, the exams that I'd brushed aside as though they didn't mean a thing to me. Why should I take exams when I had a good job? But then I thought that if I got sacked or the business went bankrupt, then where would I be with no qualifications? So I did bother with the exams and walked away with two 'O' levels, one in English and one in art. I was very pleased to get art because it was the only one I worked hard for. I love art and so I used my ability to show what I could do. I was hoping to go to art college if I hadn't got the hairdressing job. I was also interested in being a designer if I hadn't got into hairdressing.

I was halfway through my sixteenth year now. I was slowly learning the art of growing up, especially with a full-time job which was hard work. I was also trying to handle money properly. It was not to be though. The day I got my first wage packet, I couldn't stop spending money as though it grew on trees. I just blew it on make-up, records, clothes and going out to nightclubs, the typical things teenagers spend money on.

Now fashion makes great demands on people; obviously, you have to keep up with it. I do seem to dress better than I have done for years. I do tend to buy rather expensive clothes so it's no wonder that I never have any money to put away in the bank, which is pretty stupid of me.

One of the things I like about my job is that I meet different sorts of people each day which is very interesting. Styles have become very artistic within the last year. Make-up has also become a bit adventurous now. I sometimes do go over the top a bit, but I love it and I always change it every day, the colours and the style. I also love doing my hair in outrageous styles when I go out. I've got long, black, thick hair so when I backcomb it so, it looks like I have masses of hair.

There are some pretty good nightclubs about nowadays; I've been going to one in particular since I was fifteen. My mum didn't find out till I was seventeen which makes me feel pretty guilty. I never told her; I thought I was old enough and mature enough to go into nightclubs at fifteen. I prefer going out during the weekdays especially on a Wednesday night. People think that only weekends are better for going out but I totally disagree; I have a good time on a Wednesday with my mates down at the Phonographic which is the nightclub we go to. Also there are changes which have improved nightclubs nowadays. Teenagers seem to be more confident. It used to be that a group of you went into the nightclub together and the same group came back out again all stuck together. Now teenagers tend to spread out a bit and do talk to others instead of amongst themselves.

I think a lot more nowadays, thinking about others and not myself all the time. Being eighteen has altered my attitude to life; these six years of growing up have broadened my horizon as to the future, a future that I'm sure will be a good one if I go about it in the right way. Maybe in the years to come I'll be looking back on my teenage life, a life that I've enjoyed so far. I suppose being a teenager is the best memory you can have, a memory that will never fade.

VICKY BASS ◀

Birchington, Kent

'We regret to inform you that you have not been selected for interview . . .' Christine did not have to read any further, she knew what was coming next. They would say how they would put her name on their files for future vacancies, followed by a perfunctory, 'Good luck with your job hunting.' She had received a number of these standard letters since obtaining her 'A' level results, and was beginning to think there must be something wrong with her.

Christine had felt proud of herself when the results had come through, and she imagined the world would be crying out to employ her, but she had since become disillusioned. Employers were not interested in her 'A' levels, they wanted experience, a car owner, someone over the age of twenty. The fact that she could write reams on Louis XIV's foreign policy was irrelevant.

The following September, Christine began a one-year secretarial course. If someone had told her a few months back that she would be at college learning shorthand, typing and the wonders of the lateral filing system, she would have laughed in their face. The last thing she wanted to be was a secretary; with stiletto heels clicking on polished floors and typewriters clacking in grey offices – no thank you! However, typing would be a useful skill,

82

she told herself, and at least she would escape the dole queue.

The following June, she finished her course with the final exam over; she pulled the screwed-up typewriter cover out of the drawer for the last time and placed it over her typewriter, as if suffocating it. Christine and her clique of friends breezed out of the college gates, without looking back and went off to McDonald's to exchange phone numbers and addresses over hamburgers and milkshakes. Later, Christine went home on the hot crowded bus, squashed between large old ladies in polyester dresses discussing the weather, and thought optimistically about her future . . .

The following day was signing on day, 9.15 a.m. at box two. As usual, the girl asked if she had worked, and as usual Christine replied that she had not. She realised that a lot of people would look upon her as a scrounger, having a paid holiday at the expense of taxpayers; but it was not like that at all. She had a brain, and she wanted to use it, and besides, who takes only £23 spending money (her dole allowance) when they go on holiday, she mused.

Her next stop was at that well-known thriving hive of enterprise, the Job Centre. Christine scanned the cards, 'What on earth's a horizontal borer?' she thought as she looked at one vacancy; she could think of a few people to fit that description quite well. Squeezing past the other two people in the Job Centre, she managed to get back outside and went off to buy a newspaper, arriving back home in time for 'Rainbow' on TV. Zippy and George were discussing the various uses of loo roll insides. After 'Rainbow' came 'The Sullivans'. Christine turned off the television and went upstairs to listen to her radio and read the paper. She listened to the radio quite often, usually to the local station, as they advertised job vacancies over the air. She was amazed to read in the paper that some boys from a certain university were considering awarding Samantha Fox with an honorary degree for her outstanding success. 'Well girls, throw away those textbooks, forget those essays, just flash your assets to the world if you really want to get on,' she said to herself. There was also a helpful article by someone who had decided that the lack of jobs was all in the mind, and went on about how they cycled to work for forty years, eight days a week on a bike with no saddle. She threw the paper down and lay back to listen to the radio. Presently, the job spot came on.

The first job mentioned made her sit straight up and listen. There was a vacancy at the radio station for a reporter. This was just the job Christine wanted. She enjoyed writing and liked meeting different people, she would also be able to use her acquired typing skill. She scribbled down the address. The adrenalin began to flow as she began to compile her letter of application. She was very pleased with the result and hurried off down to the town to get her curriculum vitae photocopied and to buy some quality bonded notepaper and envelopes. 'This is it,' she thought as she posted her letter.

For the next few days, she thought enthusiastically about the job. She gabbled away to her mother about how it would not be just an ordinary nine-to-five job, as she would be out meeting people. When her giro cheque arrived she cashed it immediately and went to one of the expensive dress shops and bought herself a new dress for the interview. She used up nearly all of her two weeks' dole money but was pleased with the result. The dress suited her, making her look older and very self-confident. She pinned all her hopes on the job and woke early every morning to wait for the letter which would tell her when her interview was to take place.

On the day the letter came, she woke early as usual and switched on the radio, listening for the postman's footsteps up the garden path. At 7.36, she heard the letters slap on the doormat. She went to the top of the stairs and looked down. There it was! A long crisp white envelope, she knew it was hers, it stood out from the other two small brown envelopes. She ran down and snatched it up, her hands shaking. She sat on her bed and tore open the envelope.

Hot tears of desperation and self-pity welled up in her eyes then cascaded down her face. She stared at the sharp black letters on the crisp white paper, they seemed to mock her. Christine screwed up the letter and threw it on the floor. She then wrenched her 'interview dress' out of the wardrobe and flung it in a crumpled heap in the corner.

The screwed-up letter gradually began unfolding. It was creased and misshapen, like a malevolent laughing face. She could still read the words from where she was sitting. 'You have not been selected for interview.'

JULIA BELL ◀

Dyfed

An imaginary day in the life of yet another nobody . . .

The alarm clock rang. I swore and groped for the 'off' button. Light filtered through the grimy lace curtains. It was past nine already. I switched on the radio. It was one of those temperamental devices, designed to work on a mixture of brute force and gentle persuasion. Music poured from its speakers, a jolly tune which was currently topping the charts. All electronic, with a deep reverberating bass line and the singer squawking as if he were being strangled. I burrowed under the blankets, creating a cocoon for myself. Five minutes more was all I asked. An hour later a somewhat bedraggled butterfly emerged. The room was a disaster. Yesterday's clothes flung in a heap on the floor, empty Coke and lager cans spaced between piles of books and magazines, and dirty plates piled high in the sink amidst toothpaste, flannels and soap. My stomach churned. This was the squalor I would have previously condemned. It was a defilement of my self-respect. The decor was no better. Paint peeled from the walls in long strips revealing the plaster underneath, brown stains across the ceiling where the roof leaked, and the windows were cracked and covered in a layer of grime inches thick. The furniture comprised a table, a sink, a wardrobe and a bed and of course two chairs. An ancient Baby Belling and a kettle sat on the table; and all this for forty-five pounds a month. It was daylight robbery but I wasn't in a position to complain.

I boiled the kettle, making myself a cup of grey tea in a chipped 'I love Brighton' mug. Actually I hate the place but it was the only mug I'd got. I toyed with my cereal, forcing myself to eat the unappetising mush, telling myself that it was a wicked waste of money to throw it away. I looked at the room. I was going to tidy up, if only to satisfy my own conscience. I attacked the plates in the sink vigorously, until a pile of sparkling crockery sat on the table. The books and magazines were an easier task. A case of pushing them under the bed – 'out of sight, and out of mind', and out of the way. I soaked my dirty underwear in the sink, and packed the other clothes into a plastic bag to take to the launderette. I made my bed, giving the bedclothes a liberal squirt of my best perfume to cover up the smell of sweat and general human being. They hadn't been changed for months, just another thing I had meant to do but hadn't. The place still depressed me, and grabbing my laundry and handbag I left, carefully locking the door behind me before dejectedly descending the stairs.

The launderette was a dreary place. Its floors were coated with a constant layer of filth: orange peel, cigarette stubs, empty chip papers and crisp packets. I shuffled past the portly proprietress, who favoured me with a hostile glance. I suddenly felt very lonely. I'd been here a year already and still I hardly knew anyone. It was hard, I reflected, pushing four ten-pence pieces into the slot, people here were so insular. Strangers were anyone and everyone outside their own little empires. This was her patch, her launderette and I was infringing on her territory. I wasn't one of her six kids screaming for things she couldn't afford. I wasn't the one who had to cope with her husband, drinking away the profits. I didn't live in her squalor, I lived in mine. We were the same, yet worlds apart. The wash finished and I grabbed the clothes, glad of something to do, and bundled them into the tumble-dryer.

It was all very well the government telling me to get off my backside and do something for myself. There *is* nothing to do. Give me something and I would willingly do it. Education. That's a joke in itself. As for the teachers, their policy is 'Do as I tell you, not as I do', which they use as an excuse for penalising you for smoking when they smoke themselves. I don't resent authority, but I find it hard to obey those who demand respect rather than earn it. How to make young people evade school in three easy lessons: start throwing your weight around. I've been through the system, and I left, without any remorse, at sixteen, with no qualifications, no hope and no work. I'm an outcast among my own people. Look at me! Seventeen already and what am I doing? Living off innocent taxpayers' money, that's what. I sighed. Despair was nothing new.

I made my way aimlessly up the High Street. I peered in the window of one of the fashion shops, envying the girl dressing the window. She was fitting long orange jackets on turquoise skirts with splits onto naked models. Every clashing colour imaginable seemed to be at the height of fashion. I grinned at myself, paltry in comparison with my faded jeans, mauve pixie boots and a navy sweatshirt with a hole under the arm. Fashion was too fickle and expensive to keep up with. I wasn't going to fork out thirty pounds for a jacket that would be out of fashion by the time I'd saved up enough money to pay for it.

Mum used to buy me all my clothes, but that was before. Before the Big Argument. It was all over the problem of leaving school. She wanted me to stay on and take my 'O' levels, and I wanted to leave at the earliest possible moment. We'd had long drawn-out arguments, the outcome of which had been my saying, 'I'll run away then. You can't stop me. I'll show you I can cope on my own.' 'Well, go then! Go! But you're not staying under my roof anymore.' And so I left. Defiance, the teenage foible, had let me down again. I shrugged, it was too late now, I've got to prove, if only to myself, that I can cope on my own. Even if it means turning to the final solution . . . prostitution. Ugh! The very word makes me shudder. I think I would have to lose all my self-respect before turning to roam the streets.

My teenage years, as you have probably gathered, were hell. Continual conflicts with my mother made it unhappy to say the least. It is hard though. Teenagers are made to follow the crowd, and made to conform. Just one big bunch of aimless people, straining at the leashes of parental constraint, while reaching for the elusive goal of adulthood. We are expected to rebel, like popular music, like fashion and to generally be the same as everyone else. Parents expect rebellion, and teenagers rebel almost as a duty, as if it is expected of them. Those who are different are mocked and ridiculed, made to feel outcasts – but just look who's leading the crowd – those who are different. Boy George for one, it used to be the big thing at school to dress in the same way as he did. I remember one girl. She never wore fashionable clothes, she had acne and glasses and her ambition was to become a concert pianist. They derided her and frequently ignored her as a 'weirdo', but they're laughing on the other side of their faces now, she came runner-up in the Young Musician of the Year! Teenagers have, in my opinion, got to lose the shackles of conformity, they are all so scared. Scared of what others will say, chained to what others do. It seems so stupid when looking at it from the adult side of teens, and yet when you are in the middle of it, it is deadly serious.

I passed the electricity shop, the television screens flashed, mute the presenters' mouths moved up and down. I haven't watched the television for months, perhaps I'll save up and buy a TV – but then again I might not. I just don't know.

Later, back in my flat, I sat contemplating my situation. What am I to do? I can't go on day after day doing nothing. I want to run home to my mother and fling my arms around her and apologise – the prodigal daughter returns, but my pride won't let me. I might make it on my own, who knows? I am just another social security number, another one of the three million headaches of the Prime Minister. Perhaps things will change, optimism will always suffice for a few hours. I have got to look beyond tomorrow, today won't last for ever. I might get married, I might find a job, I might even go home . . . and then again, I might not.

I lay back on my bed, the springs creaked under me. I stared at the brown patterns on the ceiling and felt deeply frustrated. Life, a pointless game of charades, where you spend half of your life trying to be older than you are and the other half trying to be younger. As for me? I will continue to exist, another insignificant nobody, with no hope, no qualifications, and no job. I yawned, roll on tomorrow.

BOYS, BOYS, ◀ BOYS – AND GIRLS

Headingley, West Yorkshire

I never really fully understood what was meant by adolescence. It seemed to me, from what people had said, to be a time when the rebelling teenager tore down his or her parents' ideals. Yet now I realise adolescence is a period when you find your sexual identity, and it is not altogether a good experience. I find even now at sixteen, I can have big bouts of depression, and sometimes complexes about trivial things. Yet many girls of my age have hang-ups about things other people see as pathetic. Reading the problems of teenage girls writing to a magazine like *Just Seventeen*, you can criticise them and say they should worry about something better. To a point though, it is the media's fault.

For instance, everyone has an idea about the time in a girl's life when she should have a boyfriend. If she does not, and does not appear to have any interest in boys, some people will regard her as an outcast, a late starter, trying to put aside other thoughts.

Not having a boyfriend and not being sexually attracted to any particular boy worried me. I tortured myself, crying, being moody, jealous of other girls, becoming paranoid about my looks. I was not being vain, trivial, I was questioning myself, trying to rebuild myself into something I was not. Why? Because the people around me, the media, i.e. television, said I should have gone with a boy. This stage of adolescence, when I was obsessed with my looks, has gone, but my friend has it as part of her character. She says she feels insecure about boys and needs fairly frequently to be told she is attractive.

Actually going out with boys has affected some of my

friends, their personalities, and their ideals. They had ambitions, and now it seems they would be happy to be housewives. They are content to be bossed around, treated like the little woman, and are compensated for this by being told they are pretty. This maddens me because they begin not to have a mind of their own, and boys generalise about girls because of the latter.

From this, I have realised I want to have an identity, be an individual as far as I can. I feel I have a lot of feminism because I object to the way girls are still treated. At school, particularly, I object to the barriers teachers tend to create, for instance a teacher who asks for 'two strong boys to carry a desk'.

The majority of the girls I know are going against the system. Teenage girls want individualism. They want to get to the top in the profession they choose, or exam they take, and are undeterred by the eventual harassment they accept men will give them. If anything, this seems to make them all the more determined. I still feel, though, that this country will see an upheaval in the traditional role of the woman, and a new generation will emerge whereby women and men are equal. Possibly another fantasy of the teenage mind?

DANIELLE HOMBURG

Leeds, West Yorkshire

I was eleven in 1980, the start of a new decade, the start of a new school, the start of life – or so I hoped. By 1990 I'd be twenty-one and an adult. There seemed so little time to change so much.

I don't suppose I was particularly pretty when I began high school, though I was convinced that that long awaited puberty would miraculously change the ugly duckling into the beautiful swan that the fairy tales always promised I'd become if I waited long enough. I detested myself then for being imperfect in a world where perfection shone out of the TV screen. I strived for maturity in my childish demands for a bra (though I had no chest), and prayed daily to God to let me become a woman, however uncomfortable my friends said it was. My grandma said that everything would happen in due course – grandmothers are always right.

By the standards set by those around me, I was late in discovering there was more to boys than inkstains and football. I was probably thirteen when I experienced my first crush, and how it hurt to be so unfulfilled and yet not to know what fulfilment was. By now, all my friends seemed to be 'experimenting' whilst I could only sit and wait for the outward signs of maturity to develop.

In 1983, the magazines enthralled me with their romantic stories, whilst comforting me on their problem pages. Yes, I was normal, and everything came in due course – just as my grandma said.

It was wonderful to be fifteen in 1984. Orwell had prophesied doom and destruction but I, heedless of his warnings, fell in love. I met him on a youth-group holiday, and in two weeks I had learnt more about myself than the rest of my short life had so far taught me. I learnt love hurts, it's not all sunshine like the teenage romance books had told me. It didn't end in that magical first kiss, but in tears and pain and rejection. I lived, surprisingly, and over my next year stumbled over a variety of short-lived romances and many brief encounters. Mixed in somewhere with these explorations, I guess I started growing up.

Perhaps it was part of the social crowd I circulated in, or perhaps it was the time I grew up, 1985, that demanded I should have long lists of my conquests, and should be able to answer, confidently, the most embarrassing questions like 'How far did you go?' Something in me enjoyed the excitement of the chase, the looks, the subtle gestures, the light-headed laughter, the clichés. Like a spider watching out for her next kill, I waited for them to fall for my charms (supplied mostly by a Martini bottle). I liked the phone calls, the shy requests and my tactless refusals. I hated hurting them, yet I refused to be laid so naked to emotional pain again. I had cried once, felt strength of feeling which I couldn't understand, and as we do when we burn ourselves once, dared not go so near the fire again – not yet.

Love took second place for a while to exams, failure of which, I had been warned, would lead to an unfulfilled life in an office or at a kitchen sink. And that wasn't the life for me. I wanted to be somebody, society demanded I became important, self-satisfied, immensely popular, with a figure like a Barbie doll and hair that would make the girl in the Timotei advert want to wear a wig! I wasn't academically unintelligent, yet life had to realistically broaden out my horizons before I could hold any hope of fulfilment in the years to come. The dream romance still hovered over my shoulder, yet in front of my eyes stood my future and values which I began to realise were immediately more important that the gratification of having a boyfriend. Instead, I found the closeness of a girlfriend, intimacy without the necessity of make-up or false attractions? And, how good it was to really be able to talk to someone who'd been through it all so recently. The confidence of not having to impress or amuse, the knowledge that you were liked for what was inside of you.

Soon the troubles of everyday life began to register. Bit

by bit my innocence slipped away – people did steal, and rape and maim. Parents killed their children, the young attacked the old – hooliganism, terrorism and violence accompanied the arrival of 1986 and I found I could no longer close my eyes to the darkness of the night. I was too old to seek the comfort of my parents' bed, though sometimes I wanted to, and often I tried to fight my growing awareness and turned to idealism as a blinker. I became a vegetarian as I could not stand the thought of being the cause of pain to any living thing. I learnt about socialism and the belief that all people had a right to live as equals, in a world without hate and pain. I argued against nuclear energy, fox-hunting, seal-culling, and vivisection. I argued against all that I didn't want to accept, for to believe that anybody could be able to murder their own children, made me suspicious of my own failings, my own hidden desires. I became seventeen at a time when my emotions were all fighting for my attention. And yet I couldn't allow myself to study every feeling, for fear that I might find in myself a trait so horribly unacceptable that I would poison my own mind with my attempts to deny all that offended society.

Gradually, I pulled myself together, reprimanded myself for having agonised over too many unpleasant thoughts. I shut my mind to that which I am still not ready to examine, and pulled myself back to that half-optimism, half-self-delusion that only a half-adult can feel.

And always in the background was love. I began to discover there was more to love than I had realised. If I couldn't find perfection in myself, then it would be difficult for me to attract society's perfect man, the Levi 501 man. Yet I know that when the time comes I'll recognise true love, and no matter how imperfect he seems to the world, I will not have 'settled the half', he will be my reward for surviving my adolescence.

In 1986, I am neither a child nor a woman, more a woman's body, filled with the dying nightmares of a child and the growing fears of an adult. And I still strive for perfection because that is what society demands of me, of all of us. I am not yet ready to accept myself as I am, or the world around me for what it is. Somewhere deep inside me I still hold the young girl's dreams of the perfect woman and the perfect man, and I can't help but wonder if maybe next year, when I'm eighteen, the ugly duckling will be transformed.

STEPHANIE J. HALL

Woking, Surrey

Relationships Stink

Relationships stink
The trouble they cause
The rows and the bitching
The fights and the wars.

And love's just a lie
That gets in the way
The rubbish that people
Come out with each day.

Relationships stink
It's all just an act
Love is pathetic
And that is a FACT.

'MAISY HAMILTON'

Kinross-shire

I'm a fourteen-year-old, one of many who never usually write to magazines or enter competitions, as to us it seems such a long shot at being printed or winning. None of my friends ever seem to win. At fourteen, I'm at the 'can't be bothered' stage where everything we set out to do is never done. When our mother says, 'lay the table', we can't even be bothered to reply; we're that lazy. I regard myself as a mature adult but to the old-fashioned parents I'm still *the kid*, which is the most aggravating name to call me. 'What would the child like to drink?' a waiter once asked my father. I wanted to turn round and say, 'Look here, matey boy, I'm an adult,' but being my usual timid self, I declined the opportunity. If I had, my mother would have turned round and said, 'Sorry, but she's at *that* age.' What is this 'that age'? My brother has been at 'that age' since he was ten and he now happens to be seventeen.

Adults don't seem to appreciate that us young teenagers have lots of bright ideas; I'm sure if we were approached, they would realise that we could give them a lot of interesting hints. To them we don't know anything.

The main things my girlfriends and I discuss is boys, boys, boys and more boys. We stay up till early hours in the morning discussing who's the sexiest, who's the hunkiest, who's the sportiest, etc, and every week we'll fancy someone different. To my parents, sex was very rarely discussed and when it was it was in the comfort and privacy of their own home. But to my friends, we openly discuss sex with no problems. We even talk to boys about sex. They say, 'Did you hear about Doreen and David, they did such and such last night,' and we reply, 'Would

99

you ever let your girlfriend do that?' An honest reply awaits us.

There is a grand total of twenty-eight in my registration class, and six say they have 'gone the whole way'. If they have, they have to brag about it. Personally, the idea of losing your virginity at fourteen makes me sick, although in a class survey only one girl said that she didn't agree with sex before marriage. My parents say that in their day and age it was unheard of.

It occurred to us when my three friends and I were discussing our main topic, sex, that the two with older sisters and no brothers spend more time on making themselves look nice than the two with older brothers. The two of us with older brothers were much closer to boys as friends, whereas the two with older sisters always had to be going out with someone.

I walked into physical education last week and one of my friends scoffed, 'Oh, how could she come to school with her legs looking like an African jungle?' To be honest, I don't mind if my legs and underarms are hairy. But that is only my opinion.

There is a lot of rivalry between friends, who can get the best-looking guy, who's got the nicest clothes. It really gets you down, especially if your income is very low. Boys tend to go for the girls with a twenty-four inch waist and 36C bra and money, but those are the ones you steer clear of as there are nicer ones who don't care about any of these things.

I truly and utterly hate having an older brother, because everything to my parents is boring the second time round. Sometimes you virtually have to yell to get noticed and when you do, you get shouted at for being rude. Your problems at school cannot be discussed because parents literally don't understand. My problem at the moment is that it's the time of the year when the football's on television and everyone's rotten to me; they say it's my fault England lost. (You see, I'm English but live in Bonnie Scotland.) One girl actually fell out with me as she said it was my fault that Mary Queen of Scots got locked up in the castle. Honestly, how pathetic can you get?

'CHRISTINE'

London

I am nineteen now and I have recently decided not to sleep with any more men. This autumn I began to let myself find other women attractive and I have realised that it is OK to do so. Truthfully, I don't think that it is any big deal whether you are straight or gay, as long as you enjoy what you do and do not let any relationship continually hurt you. I wasn't happy with sexist men or 'non-sexist men' who were just as bad as sexist ones, and I wasn't happy with heterosexual relationships, so I decided to leave them all alone. I would be celibate except that I actively prefer women to men, and I can admit that to myself now.

It started when I met a lesbian who lived in my residence at university. At first, I did not know that she was gay, but I had an idea that she might be as I sometimes saw a tall, dark, mysterious woman float silently along the corridor to visit my friend. I thought vaguely that she might be my friend's lover. After a couple of months I got talking to this woman. I told her that I felt fine now but a couple of weeks before I had gone through a real identity crisis and became convinced that I was a lesbian. I laughed and made it clear that I had sorted myself out (lie, lie) and was as straight as an arrow once again. We talked about feminist politics a bit and about lesbians, and I found it all fascinating as I had never spoken to a real dyke in the flesh before. She seemed nothing like the stereotype that I had imagined. To my uneducated eye she looked so straight and 'normal'. She managed to dispel many of the dark clouds of mystery that I had built up in my mind's eye around the image of the lesbian. I had imagined a Virginia Woolf or some other very intense, passionate woman with a husky voice who smoked cigars and had wild black hair. I had a sneaking suspicion that I might be a dyke myself, but I tried not to think about it – I tried to ignore all the memories I had of being madly in love with a girl at my school, or of fancying women. I tried, for a while, to ignore all the feelings that I had buried that told me that what I really wanted was to love women.

The woman I met at university took me to my first gay club in London. I felt extremely nervous but once I got there I liked the atmosphere and the music. I was excited about the fact that for one night at least I had found a secret, man-free world. I looked at all the dykes around me, dancing together, kissing and cuddling, and it seemed somehow totally natural. I felt at home among these women after a few hours and a few bottles of Pils. It was really good fun.

There are many political reasons why I do not like relationships with men, but to most young women I believe they are self-evident. In a society where men oppress women to such a degree, the oppressed need strong friendship and love to bind them together. When I was in a heterosexual relationship I always felt that it tended to isolate me from my friends, especially other women. I became scared of women and usually saw them as a threat to my relationship. I intend to make up for my past isolation now. I missed out on a lot of fun by having boyfriends.

Three Easy Steps to Becoming a Lesbian

1. Open your eyes. Look at the power your boyfriends have over you. Do you sometimes feel uncomfortable being subject to their mental and physical power? Why do you go out with them? Is it because they have cars, money, age and status and you feel by sleeping with them you get a share of that? It's bullshit if you think you've got power over a man because he desires you in bed. Remember rape. Can women rape men?

2. Think about the women friends and girlfriends you've lost because of men. Think of all the jealousies and hatred you've built up between you and friends over some poxy man. Think of the times you've turned down going out with girls because you wanted to see your man. Was it worth it? Is sex with men really all that great?

3. Look at men. Look at men looking at pornography. Look at what men have told women they should look like. Look at what women really look like, unadorned, natural women – beautiful and ugly. Look at macho men, using you as a status symbol to prove their masculinity. Do you find that attractive? Do you still find a heterosexual relationship attractive? Or, do you find men revolt you? Do you find other women attractive? Do you love women?

MEMORIES ◀

JENNIFER KANNAIR

London

The thing that I most remember about my early life was when I started going to infant school at the age of five. My mother had got me up very early in the morning to help me wash and dress, taking out one of my best suitable little pink dresses from my rack of dresses in the wardrobe, followed by a rolled up pair of white woollen tights grouped away among all the many different coloured ones.

My mother had told me that she was happy at the time for me to go to Westville because it saved her from going out and buying a uniform.

I had felt very excited to be starting school. I could hardly wait for my mother to finish dressing me as she carefully helped me to finish pulling up my woollen tights and lifted my pink dress and straightened it out ever so neatly. Twisting and turning I felt almost like one of my dolls nicknamed Chubby Lorinda, whom I always dressed nicely. The finishing touches would be my hair and shiny black shoes. My mother had always done my hair very neatly and secure, every day plaiting it into ponytails and sticking bows everywhere along the top and the bottom. Regardless of her pulling and tugging, my hair seemed to have a mind of its own, battling against her rough handling hands. Lastly were my shiny black shoes, which would be continually shined again and again and again. At the end my feet would twinkle and reflect like mirrors against my bright white tights.

But as my mother looked down at me and stroked my dark hair and as I looked up at her, I remember seeing her eyes darken beneath the forced smile. I knew that my mother was sad about me going off to school that morning.

Taking me in her arms she hugged me as if she would never see me again, her wet cheek joined with mine, soft and dry. As we were due to leave, she gently wiped her tear stains from my face and hers, being extra careful not to smudge the rest of her make-up.

I felt nice and warm, wrapped up in my hat and mittens, ready for my first day at school as my mother led me out into the cold winter wind. She gripped my hands so tightly that I felt as if my bones were crushing into pieces inside my hand. Walking along the street I observed every house, car and tree that caught my sight. My mother never uttered a word to me. It was as though she was a zombie in control of her own self only. Turning off a corner and walking along a quiet street, my mother pointed out part of a building saying that it was going to be my new school. It looked so big and unusual to me. I remember gazing constantly at it.

As me and my mother got to the end of the street, we could see other mothers with their children like me who were heading for the school gate clutching onto their mothers' hands tightly. But my hand held my mother's hand tightly. I was looking forward to starting school so much that I hardly took any notice of the other children's reaction to starting school. We followed the mothers and the children into the playground where there was already a big crowd of teachers, children and mothers in the centre.

Not before long I soon found myself gathered among a small group of children ready to go off with this lady who had reddy hair and was quite short and fat with a witchy sort of look. Her eyelids were almost covering her eyes as if she could hardly see. I felt so uncertain about being with her. Her eyes looked so wicked and horrible that it looked as if she could see right through a person.

Without wasting time, she had led us through into the school and upstairs along the corridor to the first room. The floors shimmered and shined like my shoes that I was wearing. The whole place smelt like a hospital, even the room we stayed in with desks neatly piled together over one side of the room. Over to the other side in the corner sat a small case filled with books, and lots of flowers stood along the window.

'Right then,' she said in a high upper voice, automatically combing her fingers through her hair and grinning in a painful way at the mothers who were standing by their children and concentrating deeply on her. 'There will be a half day for your children, because it's the first day for them, so would it be OK if you came back for them at lunchtime?'

'Oh, OK,' said the mothers looking more sad than happy. My mother walked slowly over to me, sadly kissing me quickly on the cheek and walked out of the class room. I could hear her feet echoing into the distance like horses' shoes. Trying my very best to hold back the tears from tumbling down my cheeks, I went back to my seat, grimly.

Banging the door shut after the mothers, the teacher walked back to her desk and pointed sharply at each individual to tell her their names, her eyes glowed evilly at them, as if she was flashing some bad spell about. When she finally came to me, I stumbled over my second name because her straight cold face had made me tremble with fear. I had to repeat myself a second time, I could feel my ears gradually getting hot along side my cheeks and every eye fixed upon me.

Just as I had finished speaking a knock came on the door and distracted everyone's attention. A pretty woman with long blonde hair reaching her hips. She spoke softly to us, saying she was our reading teacher, flicking her hair back

109

freely over her shoulders. She floated endlessly around the room trying to learn all of our names. She was calm and quiet with us and smiling warmly. She was our kind of teacher. The ringing of the bell sounded the end of the lesson and as I waited for my mother to come, she commented sweetly on how my pink dress looked on me and the huge bows which stuck out on my hair. The other teacher looked me from head to toe and flashed a no jealous smile at me immediately and walked outside.

Walking home with my mother, I was looking forward to school the next day, answering my mother's questions quickly and joyfully.

'CRW' ◀

Wadhurst, East Sussex

I live in a small village, in the middle of a council estate. Behind our house are some fields and a small wood. The village has no night-life, it has seven pubs, but they get boring. We used to be barred from most of the pubs, 'cause we were too young. I'm one of seven children, at home there are only four of us. I have to share a bedroom with two of my sisters, which I can tell you isn't much fun. In 1981 my gran came to live with us, because my grandad had just died and gran couldn't look after herself, she was senile. Now my brother had to move out of his bedroom and sleep on the sofa. A few months later, my brother's girlfriend came to live with us because her parents threw her out. She was only eighteen, I used to think how old she was, but now I think how young and brave she was. Now there were eight of us in a three-bedroomed house.

My gran was really nutty, she flattened my mum twice. When she went to the loo for a big job, she would wipe the mess all down the walls, or chuck it out of the window. I know this sounds nasty, but when she used to sit down the garden in the deckchair, with her cowboy hat on, we used to throw a ball at her to see who could knock her hat off first.

I was nearly fourteen at the time, a gang of kids my age and my brother's girlfriend used to hang around together. As there was nothing to do in the village, one of the things we used to like to do was knock down the cat Ginger. Nobody used to come after us, only one man who we called Noddy; we called him this because when he spoke he nodded his head. We really used to pick on him, we threw stones at his house, milk bottles as well; I feel awful for doing those things now, at the time it was fun. He called the police several times and the cops would take our names, addresses (they weren't our real names we would give) and say they would come round and question us. Our parents would kill us if the cops came round. In 1985, Noddy had his leg amputated. He wouldn't be able to hobble after us now. I do feel sorry for him now.

When the gang had nothing to do, we would go to the woods behind our houses, build a camp and a fire. We used to jump over the fire and the others used to smoke. The gang were nearly all boys, only three girls, so at school all the other kids would ask if I was going out with any of them. This made me sick; just because I went round with them, they thought we were dating.

In 1982 we were now in the third year at school. There was a summer camp in Birmingham, I really wanted to go, but my parents couldn't afford it so I talked to the teachers and they let me go for a third of the price. It was great, there were few teachers and no parents, we ran free for a week. Later on that year, my brother's girlfriend moved out, and the gang sort of faded away. Now, four years later, we rarely see each other, even though we live near each other; when we do see each other it's just a quick 'hello'; we don't talk like we used to.

In 1983 I started going out more, to discos, cinemas, pubs further afield. At first my parents didn't like my going out; then they got better. If we were out later than ten at night our parents came looking for us.

We went to Bournemouth on holiday, I really enjoyed it. I first went ice-skating down there. I couldn't get the hang of it at first, but I soon learnt. I've always wanted to play ice hockey; I think I would enjoy it. The nearest ice rink is about twenty-five miles away so I can't go very often.

This was the year we started to play truant from school. A lot of us did it, I was surprised there was anyone left at school! We also got caught several times. My mum told us off, while my dad thought it was funny. Maybe he used to do it. I know my mum did, she used to throw her school-bag over the hedge when the bus came so she would miss it.

For pocket money, I would get five pence. At the end of 1983 it went up; if I was lucky and my dad had the money, I would get fifty pence. All my friends would get about two pounds. If it was Christmas or my birthday, the other kids would ask what I got; when I told them, they would say, 'is that all?' My parents couldn't afford much. The other kids were getting things like big stereo systems.

I didn't know anything about drugs in 1983 but I was offered some. A girl at school offered them to me, they were called magic mushrooms. They just looked like ordinary mushrooms. She got them from a field behind the church, so she claimed. Some of the old gang took some, but I wouldn't touch them.

For a small village a lot happened here, there were rapes, break-ins, vandalism, stabbings, suicides, fights. I think because there wasn't much to do, all these things happened.

In 1984 at school my friends and I were known as sort of rebels. It was in the middle of my exams when suddenly my dad died. It's funny someone you've known all your life suddenly disappearing, it shakes you up bad. The doctors sent my senile gran away to a mental home the very same day; the house now felt so empty. I became very quiet, didn't go out very much and began to think things through more.

I left school and looked for work; the unemployment figures were at their highest and it wasn't easy. I was fed up with my family nagging at me to find a job. I eventually found a job in a factory. I met a girl there I knew from school, her mum had just died as well. She was the only one I could talk to about my dad's death, she knew how I felt. One day, I was with two friends, they were talking about my workmate's mother, they said they understood how she was feeling, they both had parents. So I said to them that they couldn't understand; you don't know what it's like until it happens to you.

At school the careers teachers didn't help you much, they didn't tell you what it was like in the big wide world, all they said to me was, 'How are your brothers and sisters?'

In 1985, one of my sisters was now divorced (her ex was seeing his secretary). My senile gran died. I was getting back to my old self, I went out with my workmate to loads of places. I gave up my paper-rounds and Saturday and evening jobs. I've now got a punk hairdo.

My life was becoming my own – not quite though. I once arranged to stay at my sister's one night, I was going on the train, but my mum arranged for me to go with my

113

older brother, only he didn't turn up. I wish people would stop interfering with my life; boy, was I mad.

In 1986, I began to read lots of books and watch lots of films, especially films with young American actors in. They are known as the Brat Pack. They are very talented and good-looking, I think I identify with them and the characters they play. My favourite of these films is called *The Outsiders*.

Next year we are going to America, I've been saving all year. Some of the last words my dad said to me were, 'Save all the money you can.'

Since 1981, I have idolised Toyah Willcox, she's really got my admiration. One of the Brat Packers' fathers was recently in London in a play, he is a famous actor called Martin Sheen. I'm a great fan of his and, as I don't know my way around London, I sent him a letter. A few days later he sent me a picture postcard with his autograph and a small note on the back. I really admire him for that, not many famous people do that.

I don't dye my hair much now. At school when my hair was pink the teachers told me it affected my school work and told me to wash it out. But as Toyah said in one of her songs, 'So what if I dye my hair, I've still got a brain up there.' As for ambitions, I would love to be an actress, or a writer, I've got so many ideas in my head for stories. I would also like to be an ice-hockey player. I want to immigrate to America, I told my mum that last year; I expect she didn't believe me. I think I would belong out there. My sisters argue a lot, I end up piggy-in-the-middle, I'm fed up with them fighting. I used to try and stop them, but I don't bother now.

There's not much on TV, my favourite programmes are 'Sons and Daughters' and 'Cheers'; I think the adverts are better than the programmes. I used to like living on the estate, that was when I was young, but now I hate it, everyone talks about you and stares at you. I say you can't trust anyone else. I see young children and teenagers running about and I just ache to join in with them. I'm eighteen now; although I didn't like the last six years much, here are just some of the things that happened. I would just love to be back at school and thirteen again. If any teenagers read this, make the most of your teenage years, they don't last long, but they are fun.

SAFINA JIVRAJ

London

My name is Safina and I live in London. I was born in Mombasa, which is in Kenya. I don't remember much about Kenya as I moved here when I was two years old.

At the age of eleven my dad was told he had to undergo a major heart operation, as three of his arteries were at least ninety per cent blocked due to heavy smoking. I didn't understand what that meant at the time, but later it was explained to me. From my point of view, I thought he needed the operation because he wasn't able to climb up stairs easily and even when we went for walks, he lost his breath quite quickly. The operation was thirteen hours long. It involved taking out the vein from his left leg in order to stitch it onto the blocked arteries to permit a bypass.

All of us, my mum, Saleem my brother, and I were so worried. I remember the three of us sitting down to pray for him. That night when I finally got to sleep I had a horrible nightmare. I kept seeing my dad on the operating table all cut open. I dreamt that his heart, still connected to

115

his body, was in a tray, beating and that the surgeons were laughing and mockingly starting to cut more of him away. At that point I woke in horror. I wanted to run to my mum and tell her, but I decided that it wasn't sensible as she was worried enough and this would just make it worse.

My dad stayed in the hospital for at least a month before he was discharged. When he came home, he looked much better. I remember just after the operation my dad used to go through phases when he thought he was useless, and was unable to do anything, but we brought back his confidence in himself, after which he does almost anything. Now he plays badminton very well and often goes for long walks without losing his breath. Also he has stopped smoking which is a great help. He's much happier now than before, and I'm happy for him as well.

At the age of fourteen the most embarrassing thing happened to me. One day I got on a number twenty-eight bus. I went and sat upstairs, near the window. After two or more stops, a gorgeous looking guy came and sat next to me. I thought, 'Wow . . . today's my lucky day!' All of a sudden I started getting an itch in my right leg (the one nearest to him). I tried to control it, but it got worse and worse so quickly I began scratching my leg. Somehow I just couldn't feel anything. I scratched harder and harder but still I didn't feel anything. Meanwhile, this guy sitting next to me kept turning around and giving me strange stares and was sweating like anything. Then I slowly looked down. You wouldn't believe it. Instead of scratching my leg, I was scratching his. I didn't know where to put my face, I could feel it growing into a big red tomato. I tried to explain myself, but he thought I was really weird. He got up and walked away. Ever since that day I haven't sat on a number twenty-eight bus. I never have been so embarrassed in my whole life.

116

At this present day, I am fifteen years old. If I pass my 'O' Levels in the next month the plans for my future are as follows. Firstly I shall take three 'A' Levels – maths, biology and chemistry. After I have passed them I want to go to medical school and become a homeopathic doctor, and then probably take a course in acupuncture. Well, I hope I work hard and everything goes my way . . .

MISFITS ◀

London

I sometimes wonder whether anyone, even those with the most gentle of natures, and happiest of homes, can look back over their teens and honestly say that they never once cursed that time.

I doubt I'll be able to, I'm only two years into my teens, and already the turbulent ups and downs of a rapidly changing me have sometimes left me scared, and a mite irritated that the switch from a dependent child to an adult has to be such a confusing affair. And to add to the problems, I'm a misfit.

A misfit? Well, that's the way I describe myself. If the word conjures up images of a poor soul, sitting at the back of the class, alone and rejected, then re-think for a minute: there are many ways in which one can be a 'misfit' without it being plainly obvious to an outsider. Classmates talk to me, joke with me, spend lunch hours with me, but for most (except for a few others who are genuine friends – and are also misfits!) I'm not of the same breed. The reason is simple: there are two very definite groups in my school. The first are those who like soul music bands, like Five Star, who wear expensive clothes and jewellery, and who talk a great deal about boyfriends, and whether or not Jane over there is a 'slag'. The others are those who have either a fashionable, but not dressy, style in clothes, or have a slightly studentish look about them; if I were to generalise I'd say they all seem to like James Dean, support CND, and on the whole are vegetarians! And me? Well, I sympathise with CND, and the James Dean films made a good point, and though I have less in common with the other group, with their sexism against their own sex and the

121

double standards they accept, if I wanted to I could have slipped in with either group in the first year. But the whole idea of 'fitting in' has never appealed to me. The price you pay is too high: you pay for the nights out, the larger selection of boyfriends, with your freedom. And anyway, who wants a larger selection of boys to go out with, if, when you are seen with more than one of the pack, during a relatively small amount of time, you're labelled a 'slag'? Wrong though the label may be, once you have it, it sticks like glue. There is a certain amount of the same attitude in both groups.

Other reasons as well as the boy factor make me think that you're imprisoning yourself to a certain degree by joining a group. There's clothes to have to wear in one group, and certain politics to have to follow in the other, not to mention plenty of other unspoken rules of conduct. So after weighing up the fors and againsts, I decided, like a few others, to remain almost totally myself. In doing so, it means I can cross the bridge between the two groups very easily. In fact, I *am* the bridge! I can wear scruffy clothes, join CND, and like Five Star if I want.

But being a misfit has many annoying consequences. Because you tend not to talk about your out-of-school life, it is taken as a fact that therefore you are a pure innocent little thing who has yet to experience the joys of having a boyfriend (!) It sometimes, but not in my case, is true; even if it was I tend to think, 'So what?'. You have to grow a thick skin against some of the bitches in class, who find amusement in continually criticising your hair, clothes, way of speech. If you retaliate, it's bound to cause trouble, and the amount of fuss an argument or a fight would cause is just not worth it for a few empty-headed comments on your hairstyle.

You may think that these groups give you the chance to

122

run away from old-fashioned parents and school pressure, and they do, but I don't think that they give you real freedom; there is not enough room for your own views and style. Not many people will like what I say. Many will think I'm taking a very narrow, stereotyped view, but it's not often you hear a misfit's side of the story and I'm simply trying to show how the world looks from my side of the mirror.

I'm neither quiet or particularly studious. Out of school, I've never come across anyone who thinks I lack confidence, or thinks me 'serious'. But in school they are the two things I am known for, and though I used to be a little more like that in the past, no one can be bothered to find out whether it's really the case now. It's so much taken for granted that when I recently went to a party with a friend, who, although she isn't a member of a group herself, tends to take my reputation as true to life, she was very surprised when I expressed a slight interest in a boy! Though I gave up on caring about it a long time ago, that set me wondering as to how extreme their view of me really is, and how unfair.

Maybe I take their mockery and their laughter because I know that, at the end of the day, they'll stop laughing at my apparent lack of boyfriends, my relatively hard work at school; when I have my 'O' levels and my independence, and many of them have neither, it will be my turn to laugh.

Halesowen, West Midlands

Discomfort. The shoe slips up and down, up and down. Last week it was too tight. Clench my toes and keep on walking. Follow the pavement; face the open road; risk a clash with a bright red car and emerge safely.

Eyes and a stomach walk by talking intensely to lank hair and downtown fashion. Today she is a bleached-blonde; yesterday she was a variation upon mousey. A failed attempt to bring Hollywood glamour to a working-class town. Glamour. Not with an 'I want' child that salivates at the sight of a sweet shop. Is she content with her lot? Shall I ask her? I've seen this woman every five days for the past two years and don't even know her name. Will I ever speak to her? She's gone now anyway. She isn't a person to smile at. I have a special smile rota etched in my mind, composed of people whose familiarity merits recognition. Some I exchange words with. Imagine, I, too, am drawn into conversation about gardening and the weather; the 'Let's go, Mummy' boredom of plucked-skirt childhood. Occasionally I smile at new people, usually they smile back but some don't. Sometimes I forget to smile or avoid eyes so I don't have to; not today, I want to dream. I can't afford to stop, got to keep on walking.

Oh, I want to run, but the pavement is crowded with mothers returning from depositing their children. That means I must be late, I should be at the bottom of the hill by now. Damn, damn and worse. If I run for five minutes that should make up for lost time, but I have to stop to adjust this moronic shoe.

I like walking. Some people hate it; I pass them at bus stops and weave through them in traffic jams. I think when

I walk and switch off upon reaching my destination. Today I can't think because thinking delays me by ten minutes and I haven't it to spare. Late again. Why is it that my wretched soul insists upon defying the time restrictions imposed by other people?

Run now, run for thirty seconds then stop. Always slow down when facing advancing fellow walkers. They don't understand, you see. Besides, this is an area designated to the elderly, and the elderly, I am told, are frightened of the young. Youth has the power to attack, maim, even murder. Most of all youth has the power to remind the elderly that they are so.

The realms of old age are forbidden to me; I am too weak, too maudlin, too young. Is this a common phenomenon amongst today's teenagers? Doubtless I should find that it is if I spoke to people with this link of age, but I don't, so this remains a question. Age may comfort me but I am still the child. I have the same features even. Interesting. I was always under the mistaken impression that I received a new identity upon reaching adulthood; along with this came a new body, a new face. My eyes turned blue and hair white-blonde; a life-sized Sindy doll. No, the most drastic change will take place when I die and my bones reveal themselves. My teeth shall be the one remainder, misshapen and more apparent in death; a reminder that this corpse is the girl that was. There I shall lie, more vulnerable because all is exposed, but less so for there is no flesh to puncture, feelings to hurt, eyes to cry, or mouth to scream. I am brooding again. Wallowing in my own mortality; self-pity steals the show. Christ, how depressing, the thought of death on a warm spring day. Spring is the season of vitality, life; but then again I always did prefer autumn.

My breathing becomes heavy, my legs begin to ache as I climb the hill. The powder whose application rendered me

125

the loss of five minutes from my schedule, has been absorbed into my skin and replaced by warm droplets that reappear as quickly as they are wiped away. Two years of training has produced a body fit enough to walk the breadth of this hill quickly, but to run it . . . I slow down.

The burnt toffee smell of factories ahead reaches me; an invisible reminder of my exact location. The time, 9.06 a.m. Surprisingly I am carrying a watch today. Unusual for me. The clock in the Post Office window is ordinarily my pacer. Today I possess Time's keeper itself; a slim gold-plated 'lady's' watch, the unwanted present of another already too familiar Christmas day. Once the magic of Christmas made any present fantastical, but now, that same present must be magic itself to produce the old excitement; a unicorn please, Santa dear, oh, and a day ticket to the Elysian Fields would be nice. But I received a watch, an object to be forgotten each day as I leave the house. I like to be thought reckless, impulsive, without restraint, and the possession of a watch detracts from this image. Yet I acknowledge the importance of time, which means I cannot truly be any of these things; hence, my pocket guardian.

I finally reach the retirement home. Oakdene it is called, or some other such pleasantry. You can't fool me or them. A retirement home is a place where people go to die. And there is nothing pleasant about death. I have seen many funeral cars since I began to walk this way. So many, that I no longer lower my head and respectfully look away. I gaze fully and deliberately at the faces of corpse bearers. They hold no fear for me, not since I discovered their normality. They have no special secret or hidden knowledge. They are not acquainted with death, merely indifferent to it. Their uniform segregates them from society, but I wear black all the time and am not so different.

I pass the house of a friend of a friend. Luckily she is rarely visible. It is not often that I must stop and exchange embarrassed words. These are punctuated with uncomfortable silences and the shuffle of restless feet. I force myself to end it with the words of freedom that are so difficult to speak: 'Well, . . . (glance at watch) I'm late (confidential giggle) – as usual. So . . .'

I start to run now, the ground is flat and the distance short. I must make some attempt to recapture lost time. Fifteen mintues late; if it wasn't for that shoe . . . I shall arrive obscenely sweating and Belisha flushed. I am so hot. A winter jumper provides my cover for a warm spring day. I never wear traditional summer clothes, I would rather suffer the heat. They reveal the flesh you see, and I am too fat beside a mass of sylphs. Aside from that, my skin is persistently and undesirably pale. It refuses to succumb to the charms of the most seductive sun, and emerges chaste, untouched, undesirable. I admit defeat in this area, but my figure is another matter. From tomorrow I shall eat just one light meal a day, anything more is sheer indulgence. Once slim I shall wear summer clothes with everyone else. Superficially I shall appear the same despite internal differences.

I pass through the gap in the barbed fence – the back entrance to the college, suitable for late offenders like myself. I increase my pace for the benefit of Teacher. I am exposed here, visible from the classroom window. No time for abstract thoughts now, just reproaches. I curse myself as I imagine the class, the unit, sitting there, easily distracted by my late entrance. I shall be subject to their unquestioning gazes for a full minute, before they lose interest and look away. I shall try to control my disruptive, loudly audible breathing, edging past Teacher, with each step an apology. He never looks my way or breaks his flow

127

of speech. I do not exist. I shall pull out a chair (noisily). I shall drop something (inevitably). Stoop to pick it up, and fall against the chair (more noise). I shall finally sit down, turning redder, still redder. I must explode, I must, I must. I feel the stares without raising my head. What do they think of me? I can't help it, I can't. My heart shall beat loudly; each pound declaring: 'I am here, I am here.' I shall avoid looking at anyone, arrange my hair around my face, attempt to obliterate my presence while my beating heart and squeaking chair mercilessly reassert it.

I reach the college doors. They are glass, and through them I see many people inside. They stand in groups, talking, laughing. They have no lessons this period, mine is partly over. I place these people in background focus and concentrate upon the doors, trying to brace myself to enter. After all, I am always late; one more time will make no difference, everyone is used to it by now. Now, one more time. The people inside look at me, then each other and laugh. The pounding engulfs me. It's no good, I can't do it.

I turn and walk away. My foot aches with the effort of staying attached to a loose shoe. Tomorrow I shall be early.

FEELING ◀
DIFFERENT —
AND ANGRY

'SIMONE BLACK'

Birmingham, West Midlands

Am I mad for not wanting
to conform to the rules?
a woman's place is in the home
what claptrap . . . whoever wrote
that should be shot.

What is the rule?
What are the rules
for this society? . . . I want to do
a lot of things
I'm not supposed to do . . . because
I'm a woman.

Brain surgeon, pilot, go to the
moon . . . what are little girls
made of? Sugar and spice
and all things nice.

What about pain and
loneliness . . .

What are little girls made of?
Steel and stone
blood and bone
Sticks and stones may
break my bones . . .

but not my soul.

'K.F.N.' ◀

London

I moved to England from the Middle East just as I was entering my teenage years. It was an unfortunate time to move because as well as the 'culture shock' of adjusting to London, I had all the problems facing most other adolescents. I am never quite sure which of the two I should blame for the long periods of depression which epitomise my teens; it is probably adolescence, as I often see others my age suffering from it too.

Many of my friends get their enjoyment from going out to discos and going on shopping sprees. These outings have never interested me. In fact, I used to think that there was something wrong with me for not being the same as everyone else, but I now realise that most teenagers feel different from others, whether they really are or not. In most cases it is harmless, but it is sad when a certain difference becomes so marked that it gets labelled as 'freaky'. Teenagers can be very cruel to one another, but most of us know when we have been unfair and we are quick to apologise.

It is important to learn the art of apology early on to ensure a large group of friends. Looking back, I feel as if I spent most of the last few years on the phone to 'best friends'. I can't even remember the majority of the many telephone conversations, they were mostly about teachers at school, or about other girls (I have already said that teenagers can be very cruel), but I know that they were an essential part of most evenings. For me, it was always essential to have a best friend quite apart from my normal circle of friends, although I had different ones at different times.

I was never capable of coping with two best friends at the same time. That must be due to a great fear of being left out. I love belonging to groups, just for the sake of 'belonging'. That was why I joined the Girl Guides. I always enjoyed wearing the uniform and joining in on the many group activities. This had a side effect which disturbed me throughout my teens: I have always had to keep my Guide activities a secret from my schoolfriends. I did not want them to regard me as a 'square' who knits blankets for old ladies; to be 'square' is nearly as bad as being a freak.

During the eighties, a great problem has been keeping up with the many trends that come and go. I found that the best solution for me was to follow as many of them as would make me seem acceptable or normal, without following so many that I would be known as a clone. It is a difficult balance to achieve, but it comes easily with a bit of practice. The one thing which I have never taken to has been the adoration of pop stars. I do not like the idea of a stranger's face staring at me from my wall in the form of a poster, and it would greatly pain me to be 'in love' with a man who is already chased by thousands of others.

I may not appreciate the charms of pop stars, but at least I enjoy most of their music. I try to go to lots of concerts and I play my stereo as loudly as my parents can bear. Electrical equipment such as my stereo and the telephone, along with the permanent mess in my room, are the source of the majority of arguments between my parents and me. It is a shame that most teenagers find it so hard to get along with their relations because it is a time in their lives when they need them most.

A lack of communication at home, and not feeling needed, may have disastrous effects on a confused teenager. I think that they are a major cause of many of the serious problems which confront us today, like the increase of young smokers, drug-users, and glue-sniffers. These are ways for a youngster to belong to a group. I find it very difficult to be part of a minority of non-smokers in my class; between a group of smokers and a group of Girl Guides I prefer to belong to the latter. I may be 'square', but I'm a healthy 'square'.

Like most adolescents, I have many complaints against society and life in general. Most of these last a short time, but my main grumble has bothered me for a very long time: the education we receive in England. For a start, a majority of school leavers at the age of sixteen are far too immature and inexperienced to look for a job which should last them for a great deal of their life. I do not blame the school leavers, it is very tempting to be free of school and the endless exams, especially when there is dole-money waiting for the jobless, unlike in many other countries. All that is offered to those who stay on at school are 'A' levels. Instead, I think that there should be an option between them and a series of practical courses, in computing for example, and then the school leaving age could be raised to eighteen. In this way people would leave school more qualified for jobs on offer.

There are also teenagers who find themselves over-qualified for jobs. They aim too high, preferring to be on the dole rather than take a job which they find to be below them. And another group consists of those who want to become famous in whatever they do. Throughout my teens I longed for fame in whatever I happened to be doing, from a particular sport to acting. It was not a great deal of money which I was after, so it must have been because of a need to be liked and accepted, the same reasons why it has always been important to me to be part of a group of people.

KAUSER PARVEEN

Halifax, West Yorkshire

My name isn't exactly easy to pronounce
But then again it isn't surprising is it?
I have quite light coloured skin
(with the occasional spot or two).
I have dark eyes and dark hair.
Does that make me different from anybody else?
Simply because I'm Asian?

My parents are both Asian.
My religion is Islamic.
I have to wear our traditional clothes,
which are quite expensive, but
to the English people
they're nothing but junk.
'Paki, wog, nigger, Andygandy'
are some of the names Asians get called.

I may have the same sounding surname
    as Simon Le Bon's wife,
Yasmin Parvenah, but
does that make me a relation or something?
Does colour matter?
I adore Scott Baio, Zola Budd and Victoria Principal.
Aren't I allowed to like people who are white?

To me it seems the door to the white people will always be
    open —
for opportunities like jobs, work, fame, fortune,
Unlike to us Asians.
It will always be . . . ?

When we talk about racial prejudice we mean aggression towards people of another race. A subject which I have always felt at heart with because it affects everyone who is Black, Asian, Afro-Caribbean – or even an immigrant from another country. All these names are used to describe black people in Britain.

Even today you'll find Asians who have suffered racial prejudice and humiliation of all kinds. Yet nothing has really been done about it. We all know that politicians have sat down and tried to solve this problem. And a considerable amount of thought has been put into it, but there has been no result. It's about time something was done, because as an Asian I have suffered, but I'm fighting back. Like Madonna says in her song 'Over and Over' – 'It doesn't matter who you are, It's what you do that gets you far, And if I fall I get up again now, Over and Over.'

That's what I believe in and carry on believing in until proven different. I believe that everyone is equal no matter who they are or what colour they are.

Being an Asian at school I encountered prejudice which I thought was of a different kind. No one would even talk or sit next to me, perhaps there was something wrong with me – and there was. I was coloured. Did the colour of my skin make all the difference? In certain cases it did.

A few years ago I was so shy that I would not even answer my name on the register, but now I've overcome my shyness and am fighting back. If anyone calls me a 'nigger, coon, wog or a Paki' I'll argue right then and there. Despite all the publicity I receive from my friends saying that I've got guts, it isn't a question of guts. If you are proud of being black, then fight back for being black. You just give me the chance before a court, over and over until I finally succeed. If anybody calls me anything, I'll give them a warning, then complain to the member of staff present. If nothing is done,

I'll walk out of the lesson without permission, and go straight to the Headmaster. If no action is taken, then I'm going to take the situation into my own hands and solve it with what I think is best, and not bother with what other people say or think because it's what I think that's important. I don't care if I get suspended because to me it's just one of those things. By then, I hope to receive publicity from the national press and from then on I'll take steps as it comes.

I totally oppose the apartheid system in South Africa. There will be no real peace until all the people have secured human and political rights. The system is evil and self-defeating. Blacks are treated like second-class citizens. It is still illegal for blacks and whites to marry. What is wrong with two human beings who are in need of each other? There, whites have always ruled and have first priority in everything.

In 1978, the future Prime Minister, Margaret Thatcher, said people are really afraid that this country might be swamped by people with a different culture. I feel like coming face to face with that woman and showing her the present situation. Being black can be hard, especially in today's society with both pride and prejudice to face. But those who should and need to be mentioned are Dr Martin Luther King who was assassinated in 1968 as he was about to head a poor people's march in Washington. Pele the Brazilian footballer who was an international star at sixteen, scoring over a thousand goals in first-class football before he was twenty-nine. Farhath Malik, the Asian girl, who was discriminated against, for wearing trousers and took her case to court and WON! Mohammed Ali who won the world heavyweight title. At the 1968 Olympic Games in Mexico, two athletes gave a black power salute although there was plenty of protest against it.

It may not just be prejudice on account of colour, but of religion or custom also. National Front offends many people and often provokes a violent backlash from groups who oppose them. NF signs are daubed all over houses of Asian families who are afraid of having their families a victim of racial discrimination.

Asians today are prouder than ever before because being black isn't something you should be afraid of. You can't judge anyone by their colour or appearance, although people do.

I feel very strongly about this subject and have every right to because, like I said, EVERYONE IS EQUAL.

'KARINA'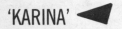

Potters Bar, Hertfordshire

Being a teenager? I'm not sure I know what it means. Can't say I ever feel like one – more like a sort of 'intrusion' in life, you know – as if I don't belong. I think it can be nice or horrible but never ordinary. For me it's horrible. You know what the hardest thing about being a teenager is? Accepting yourself. Telling yourself, 'Look, this is *you*, this is *your* body, *your* mind and you're stuck with it for the rest of your life, whether you like it or not.' The second hardest thing is accepting others, accepting the world. I want to change things. I want to help the poor, I want to ban the bomb, I want us all to live in harmony, black, white, yellow, blue, whatever. I want to make my impression on the world, on this cold and bitter and confused place I live in. You see, I want to be remembered.

The place I live in is a dump – it's not what you'd

probably call a dump, but I call it a dump. It's boring and it's middle-class and it's a little suburb with OAPs on scooters. And you know why I hate it so much? Because it scares me, it scares me to death, it seems to represent everything inside me – middle-class, boring.

School? I hate it. I loathe it, I dread it, I despise it. Why? Because I'm not in the 'In' crowd. Sometimes I get the feeling that my whole life's going to be like that – yearning to be 'in' and always missing. Drowning in self-pity, aren't I? But I'll tell you one thing – it can be quite constructive (or destructive); just fuel all that pity you're feeling for yourself into anger. It'll make you so mad, you'll *have* to do something. Back to school, though. It's one big stupid farce. It's the bitchiness and the inherent cruelty of kids; it's where you learn about the intricacies of social-standing and the colour of skin. But you know what the worst thing about school is? It's when you realise, finally, after God knows how many days of RE and maths and fighting and crying, that it's no different out there in that big, bad world you're always hearing about. That's how it's always going to be.

There's really not much to tell about my life. I'm the youngest kid and I have two sisters and we all live in a cosy little semi-detached. Miss Average incarnate. Get up at eight, walk to school, walk back, watch TV – all the soaps of course, you name it, I watch it – and I'm asleep by ten. Doesn't that sound thrilling? And I'll tell you something else too – my life is one big diet. Oh, I'm not anorexic – God knows I wish I was – I'm a 'compulsive eater'. Sounds impressive? It isn't. You know what it is? It's greed, just pure greed, plain and simple. But let's change the subject.

My first (and last) date. You're wondering how a girl like me manages to get anyone, right? Well, you're wrong you see. I like dressing up. So there are some advantages in

139

having two sisters. Anyway, I went to a disco and I met a boy and he asked me out and I said yes. The eagerness with which I accepted, no, snapped up his invitation, straightaway, just like that after ten minutes of simple talk. I can't believe I was so desperate. He wasn't even that great. Me, with all my big ideals and talk, falling for him. It's hard to talk about. I still feel so bitter and so ashamed of myself, of my lack of pride in myself. Anyway, we went out the very next day and you know what happened? Nothing. He was engaged! All he wanted was a 'bit on the side'. The rigours of the permissive society! I still hate him for that, for deceiving me and making me look a fool, but I hate myself more – for being deceived, for being a fool. But you know, I learnt something from that mess, something I'm going to remember for the rest of my life: respect yourself. If you don't, nobody else will. I think about that when I try to ignore my mother's taunts.

You know, sometimes I get so depressed I could kill myself. But I never will. See, I want to change the world – God how feeble that sounds. When I was a kid, I wanted to be the first woman on the moon. Somebody beat me to it – c'est la vie! But now I feel it all slowly draining away from me: my ambition is seeping out of me, an ounce every month. But you have to have ambition. I despise all those neighbourhood girls I see at the cheese counter in Tesco's or at the checkout in Sainsbury's. Yes, I know, you're supposed to climb your way steadily up, reach the top of that social ladder of success. But when you finally arrive there, when you've made it after all those years of slog and sweat and tears, you're going to think to yourself – 'was it worth it?'.

Two lines of a poem by Stevie Smith really seem to sum up my life until now:

140

I was much too far out all my life
and not waving, but drowning.

I wonder what the future holds for me?

LAURI OWENS

Nailsea, Avon

A Shock of Hair

Never cut your hair,
Nothing to do with femininity.
Just
Never cut it.
Let it grow,
Deep down your back.
Perhaps hide its beauty in a twist.
For the silk, or locks, or waves
That swell from you
Might be the only
Image of freedom
You can have.

RAPE ◄

Manchester

Sweet sixteen and never been kissed. Well, not exactly, but not far from it. Four years ago: doesn't time fly? But I can tell you, a lot has happened in those four years.

Sandie's my name. To begin with, my first job. It was a Youth Training Scheme; I was a telephonist/receptionist/typist (and anything else that needed doing). I really enjoyed it though. After only three months I was told I was no longer needed. So off I went and got my second job – a cashier on a checkout till in Tesco's. I hated it. But the wages were a bit better than what I'd been on, which was £36 per week.

I only lasted eight weeks. My sister Jay got me a job in the store where she worked as a cashier/typist. It wasn't what I really wanted – I wanted a job in an office but it was better than Tesco's.

My sister's three years older than me so it was great! We started to go to pubs and clubs, really living it up. The other staff were all roughly my age; I loved it, I was bubbling with confidence and happiness.

The Red Bull was one of our regular pubs. We got mixing with about six blokes. I started going out with Johnny; he was thirty-four, tall, dark and handsome. Every Thursday, Friday and Saturday night we'd go to The Red Bull, stay till closing time, then all go back to John's house. There we'd drink wine, smoke speed and listen to Monty Python tapes. I used to get completely stoned and then end up sleeping with John. We carried on going down to The Red Bull for about six months. Then we started getting bored and found other pubs and other fellas.

I loved life then; clubs, pubs, booze and fellas; my job

was going great, everything was perfect. One Thursday night, me and our Jay went in The Staf's pub near where we worked. It was always packed near weekends. Anyway, we'd been in there about twenty minutes, then we both went to the loo which was downstairs. When I was walking downstairs I thought I felt someone pull at my skirt. I turned around and there was this tall, blond-haired bloke, about thirty, behind me. He smiled and winked at me, so I turned back and thought I must have imagined it.

We went in the toilet, and when I shut my toilet door, I got a cold shiver run down me and I froze. I had a scary feeling that something was going to happen. I didn't go on the toilet, I just stood listening. Next minute I heard the main door open and quite heavy footsteps. Suddenly a man looked under my toilet door, it was the same man who was on the stairs.

I started screaming and swearing at him. By this time Jay was shouting, 'What's happening? What's going on?' I came out of the toilet, crying. After I'd told Jay what had happened, we went upstairs and she told me to point him out, but he'd gone. We went to the bar and I got a double vodka and orange, I felt really shook up. We left early that night, about 10 o'clock.

Jay was leaving her job that year, in October. We had a leaving party for her in work, then all piled into The Staf's pub. It was a really good do, and afterwards I decided to go to a club with my friend Jane. We went to a club called 'Bunnies'. We ended up copping off with these two Iranian guys. The one who I was with, Kameal, was twenty-one. He seemed really nice; he bought me loads of drinks, although he was only drinking orange. When the club closed, he offered me a lift home, saying he had a Datsun outside. I refused, as I always remember my mum and dad saying never to get in a car with any fella I don't know properly. He said he'd drop me off where he lived and then it would be cheaper in a taxi for me. So I said I would. He seemed nice and I trusted him.

How wrong I was. We drove to his house, and when we got there he asked me in for a coffee. I said no as I had to be going soon. He kept pestering, and I kept saying no; eventually he seemed to accept my answer, so we were sat in the car having a kiss and cuddle, when his hands started wandering. I pushed them away and he became really rough, pulling at my trousers. I told him to stop it, and that's when he started shouting and swearing at me. He called me 'a stupid teasing bitch' and said I was gonna get what I wanted. I was terrified. I tried to get out of the car, but he got on top of me. I was frozen with fear. Then he pulled his trousers and underpants down. I really panicked then. I was punching and shouting and trying to open the car door. He got hold of my neck, I got his hand off and bit it really hard. Then I managed to get out of the car.

I was running down a long dark road, and then I came to a main road. I must have still been panicking; I kept thinking, 'Oh God, please let a taxi come quick.' A couple of minutes later, a taxi pulled up. The taxi driver got out and he was going on, asking what had happened. When I looked down at myself, all my blouse was ripped, I think I said something about nearly being raped and to get me home quick. He said he was going to take me to the police, but I said, 'No, just take me home.'

Next morning when I woke up, I felt really rough. I didn't tell anybody. On Monday morning I just went to work as usual, as though nothing had happened. But about two weeks later, when I woke up for work, I felt very depressed; I kept crying all the time. Whereas I'd always loved my job, I started to dread going in. When I did go in I was feeling nervous and scared. When any of the men came

147

over I started trembling and blushing; what was worse I didn't know why I was acting like this. I didn't even connect it with the attempted rape.

I started staying off work sick. I did feel ill, but I think it was my nerves, not a physical illness. My mother kept telling me to go to the doctor's. When I went, he thought it was an over-active thyroid gland, as I was losing weight as well. He did some blood tests which were negative and he then told me he was going to put me on 'Ativan' tranquillisers. I think they made me feel worse. I felt numb. I stopped eating completely; I hated it when anyone looked at me and I became really paranoid. Even with my own family, I used to shake and feel as though I was going to faint.

The next four weeks were very topsy-turvy. I changed my job three times, but my manager was really understanding. I went to three different offices, doing filing, typing and all sorts; after about a week in each job, I felt as though I couldn't cope. I'd only been doing the third job two days when on the bus on the way to work, I broke down crying. My sister Jay and my other sister Lydia were with me, and I told them I wanted to go home as I couldn't face going to work. They were really upset and puzzled, as they didn't understand why. But neither could I.

That day in December 1983, I came home. I was getting thinner, and more and more depressed. I spent most of the time in bed, all over Christmas and New Year. It was awful. My mum and dad and sisters were totally bewildered.

On Friday, 13 January at 1.30 am I lay in bed wondering what I was doing, what was the point of carrying on like this. I weighed four and a half stone, and I was putting my family through hell. So I wrote a letter, and that night I took an overdose of forty-six tranquillisers. I felt so sad and sorry but that this was the only way.

I got out of bed and went downstairs. I lay on the sofa, everything went blurred and hazy; I saw Jay and then my mum. My mum got me up and then two men came in. I was put in an ambulance, I remember I kept wanting to go to sleep but wasn't allowed to. My mind goes a blank after that.

Jay told me I had my stomach pumped and was then transferred to a psychiatric hospital. I remembered my first day in the psychiatric ward. I hated it, I was scared and lonely. I kept crying and becoming hysterical, saying I wanted to go home. The first night I had hallucinations, one time I was sat on the toilet, and there was a white tiled floor with black speckles on it, I hallucinated the black speckles were spiders. I ended up on top of the toilet, a nurse found me and managed to calm me down. That night, whilst I was in bed, I saw an old woman at the end of my bed. She was telling me to follow her; I got out of bed and followed her to the sluice. She told me to go in with her, I remember shouting 'No', and crying. A nurse came again. She gave me a tablet, I think it was to sedate me.

I stayed in the ward for five weeks. Each morning we'd have to get up at eight o'clock and go for breakfast. Through the day we'd sit around and read or play cards. I made lots of friends in there, one girl, Debbie, was nineteen. We got on really well, we used to say we were going to the shops and sneak off to the pub. One time, Debbie got some drugs, so we went down the corridors of the detoxification wards and smoked it there.

Each Thursday there was a ward round. Each patient would go in a room with a psychiatrist and about ten students. I never said much, I used to feel as though everyone's eyes were on me. I was put on special milks and food. I did put weight on, though at first I used to refuse to

149

eat. They told me if I didn't they would take me to the other side of the hospital and put me on a drip.

When I was discharged after five weeks I came home and my sister Jay said the Personnel Manager from work had been in touch, and that there was a clerical job if I wanted it. I really wanted to go back to work, although I felt nervous at the thought of it.

The following Monday was my first day back. I think that was the hardest day in my life, going back to work. But I seemed to get back into the swing of things fairly well. All through 1984 I went to work each day. Every Thursday, I worked till lunch and then went to see a psychiatrist. Twelve months I saw the psychiatrist for, though I never told them what had happened, as I had four different ones. I was discharged in February 1985.

I carried on going to work, and I seemed to be building my confidence back up. In July 1985, I joined an amateur dramatic society. In November, I started seeing a married man, but it only lasted three weeks as I was feeling guilty and becoming depressed.

We missed drama over the Christmas time. When it was time to go back I was so shocked as I was really nervous. I was dreading going, it wasn't as though I had to go, but I felt as though I had to, otherwise I'd go right down.

January and February 1986 were awful months. I seemed to be going from bad to worse. I started to dread even going out of the house.

I knew I had to do something. I couldn't let it end up like last time, I couldn't put my family through that again. So I wrote a letter in detail saying everything that had happened to me. I gave it to Jay and told her to show it to our mum and dad.

When she showed them the letter, they were obviously upset, but also they said they felt relieved as now they

150

could understand why I'd done it, trying to commit suicide.

Jay suggested I go to the Rape Crisis Centre, although my dad wasn't keen on the idea. I went once and it was great. I'm going again soon.

Each day of my life passes slowly. I'm not a happy person.

I look back sometimes and think, 'Why me?' I'm twenty years old now, and three years of my life were ruined. Even now I feel very nervous when in male company, although I'm not too bad with older men.

I went through a phase about four months ago where every time I went out, I'd cop off with a bloke and then end up sleeping with him. I stopped myself, though.

I think now as I write this, I may help some young vulnerable girl like I was to be very careful. I'm very bitter; maybe one day (soon I hope) it will fade and I'll feel young and happy again, and not afraid of anything or anybody.

GILLIAN LANGDOWN

Newcastle-upon-Tyne, Tyne and Wear

Believe it or not I am actually writing this in the greenhouse at the bottom of our garden. It seems the only place I can get away from nagging parents and get a bit of peace and quiet!

I am sixteen, halfway though the 'dreaded' teen years. On the whole I have managed the 'teenage menopause' fairly well: spots, boys, parents and exams. One thing I have not enjoyed is my sudden changes of moods. Sometimes I can be as happy as larry and the next moment, depression sets in. I am depressed if I have a serious problem, but other times I just go all huffy and moody. It's unbelievable, I have just convinced myself it's part of being a teenager but I would love an explanation.

School, especially lately, has been a pressure. Exams are always on my mind, and how narrow a chance of employment is for school leavers. What's worse is revision, parents always want you to get down to revise when your favourite TV programme is in its opening stages. You feel they are just picking on you, out of spite, with that famous old line 'You will benefit in the end.' I rebelled against my parents and am now paying the price.

I find great comfort in discussing things with my dad. Not just problems, but life, feelings and emotions. Letting off steam on social problems, the things teenagers face in everyday life, the most famous being drugs, smoking, violence, sex, jobs . . . the list is endless but talking helps. I think telling my parents my views on drugs and smoking and how appalled at them I am gives them a sense of relief and confidence in me to be able to control and handle my life. Parents obviously worry, it seems only natural, all the things going on in the world, influencing their 'babies'. I am sure it will be exactly the same if I become a parent. But at present I have a tendency to argue with everything they say.

I am just looking forward to my future life, maybe in a few years I will laugh with my dad and mum about some of the things I used to say, but for now I will concentrate on exams, results and . . . a job. I think that unemployment is the main cause of most of the drugs and violence affairs. More so if a person has gone through school fairly smoothly with fair qualifications and then not being able to get a job. It must cause despair. If no effort has been made for exams or to find a job then I have no sympathy, circumstances do differ. The new YTS schemes seem to be doing a grand job, having somewhere to go after school and gaining experience is terrific. I myself enrolled on a course and am not sure what my chances will be when I leave next year.

I have not personally had any shocking experiences. Once a car pulled up and some rather shifty looking 'gentleman' asked me if I fancied a ride, but that's about it. Violence in the form of fighting has been around me, but I don't think it has affected me in any way. Attending a large comprehensive I suppose it can only be expected, but I often wonder where the offenders have picked it up. They as individuals will probably carry that aggressive streak through life; teenagers are affected by the 'adult influence'.

A problem that mostly bothers me is rape. I also hear and read about it, and used to think, 'Oh it will never happen to me.' But when a few months ago, I heard a report on the local news of a rape, literally yards from my own house, I could not believe it, but worse was to come. The victim had been my cousin, Jennifer. I never knew. Immediately I rushed to my Jenni's house. When she answered the door I could have cried. Bruises covered her beautiful face, there were finger marks on her skin that looked angry and hard, and scratches on her neck. Her face looked tear-stained, she had obviously heard the news and knew I knew. Jenni cried and cried and then talked. She had let her name go on the air because the villain had been caught and the case was in police hands. Besides, the rapist had stolen fifty pounds and Jenni's diamond ring. Seeing her in that state made me think seriously about the issue of rape. We now attend self-defence classes and Jenni's regained her confidence, slowly. When it happens to someone you love, it is totally different from reading about it. Although no one will ever feel as Jenni does, she knows so much more than us. She is a lovely girl, she has joined a rape line, which enables her to comfort girls who ring in for help and advice. If it is at all possible, something good has come from Jenni's experience.

Teenage years are what you make them (although bad experiences scar for life) and life is for living, maybe this collection of writing may help teenagers to know they are not alone and that their feelings, experiences and emotions are not strange. We've all had them and better times are on the way. We are one generation and we must help each other.

DIVORCE ◀

'MINDY'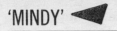

Carlisle, Cumbria

'Best years of your life,' someone once said, I suppose it could be true if it wasn't for parents. I know that sounds harsh, but imagine it: a teenage kid, going through the adolescent problems of anyone my age; boys, friends, changes physically and mentally; add to this 'O' level examinations, the piece of paper which could decide my future, school and family pressuring me into doing well (even though I realise it's for my own good); then suddenly it seemed as if my whole world as I knew it was collapsing around me and I couldn't do anything about it. I'm talking about divorce, affairs, separations, the whole horrible business rolled into one.

It started when my father announced, with some bitterness I might add, that he was having an affair. It was so unexpected, so devastating even now, looking back, I can't see how my mother managed to hold herself together. She had always been so dependent on my father. Maybe that was one of the pressures which he tried to explain to me after the initial shock.

They tried desperately to save their marriage, not once but several times, leaving a trail of bitterness and heartache behind them, but it wasn't working. My dad would sometimes leave for a few days in an attempt to gather his thoughts, sometimes returning for me, as we were always close, or maybe sometimes to relieve his guilt. Yet each time he was less like the father I had known. It was killing them both, and family life became so unhappy. I can remember many a blazing row, things were hurled, words were so blatantly said and I was stuck in the middle of them both. I tried so hard to comfort both of them. First my

157

mother, but when I was with her I was laden with guilt for not being with my father. I thought that he might think I didn't love him anymore, and vice versa. Yet as hard as I tried, I was inadequate; he finally left. Sitting home night after night, wondering if my father was all right. Many a time the thought of my dad, or my mother for that matter, committing suicide came into my mind. Why didn't he phone? I would sit there willing the phone to ring just so that I would know he was OK.

You can't imagine what it's like when you hear the bathroom door lock, wondering what my mother was doing. It seems stupid now but it was very hard at the time. The enquiring questions I constantly asked, just because I was frightened, dragged my mother down even further, lower than she was already; all she really needed was for someone to pick her up.

Then I used to think what would happen to us, what would happen to my home of comfort and all the things which I was used to and took for granted. I was soon to find out. My mother and I would go house hunting, on foot as we didn't have the car anymore. We must have walked miles. Some of the houses were too far away from things such as shops and some were oh, so very small. We really had to start facing up to the fact that we weren't going to have anything like we were used to.

The thing I wanted to do most of all was to talk to someone, no, maybe that's not true. The thing I wanted most was a big hug of reassurance. I could talk to close friends, but they didn't know how to react or what to say and that's not their fault. At first some didn't believe me as we always seemed to be a happy family, apart from the usual upsets. I didn't like to pour my heart of self-pity out to my mum as she was always exhausted and tired. She had started taking all sorts of pills, sleeping pills, pills to make her relax, sometimes even valium. I hated to see her filling herself up with that junk just so she could face getting up in the morning.

It was not long before I realised that my exams were upon me. My mother felt guilty that I had to go through them plus having everything else to contend with. She used to say, 'try as hard as you can, and if the worst comes to the worst you can always have another go.' I didn't want another go, I wanted to get them over with and hopefully do 'A' levels in the sixth form. That prospect seemed unrealistic now, I could see myself next year having to do them all again. I tried to concentrate on some hard revision but my mind just kept on wandering. It was the same actually doing the exam. Many a time I would look around me watching everyone else writing away, heads down, going through all the work they had revised in the weeks before, while my answer paper lay blank staring at me. God, parents, you do have a lot to answer for.

And how does this leave me? It leaves me with an empty feeling in my life and I feel a resentment towards marriage. At the moment I don't think I would ever get married. The whole business has put me off the idea completely. I wouldn't want to put other children through what I myself went through. Yet I suppose I will change my mind in time. Only I can't help thinking about the time I was talking to my father. I asked him if he would be happy here with us. 'Happy? No, but I'll be content.' Is that what I'll feel if I got married? So in a way I don't hate my father, I never could. I would rather he was happy. Also, I suppose I was forced into growing up quicker than I wanted to, made to face the problem with a more mature attitude.

This does sound a bit as if I'm full of self-pity, well maybe I am, but I've got feelings too and it is so very hard playing pig-in-the-middle. I know I'm not the only one who's been through something like this, but at the time it seems as if nothing is going to be quite right ever again.

Yet, I'm still here but where does everything lead to? I'm not quite sure, things are still happening, things which I don't want to know about. It gets like that, you find the more you eavesdrop and listen in the more you find out, and the more bitter you become. I interfered too much because I was frightened of the future, never giving my parents a chance to talk or argue, whatever the situation might be. So until tomorrow, another episode in my life stands open.

ANONYMOUS

Cardiff, South Glamorgan

'There's nasty,' Mary replied, after my answer to her previous question was 'nothing'.

She had asked me what I had given my father for Christmas and as I felt there should be no need to lie and why should I in any case, I answered truthfully.

Then Mary persisted, 'Why?'

I thought for a few moments. Why hadn't I given my father a Christmas present? I instantly began regretting my answer and I wished I had lied.

'Well,' I said, 'I didn't see him over Christmas, I did get him a present, but I didn't see him.'

'You didn't see your father over Christmas?!' questioned Mary bewildered.

'Ah, no.'

'Why not? Didn't you have a present from him then?'

'No, I didn't,' I answered quietly and then I forced a smile hoping to cover up my real feelings.

'Yes, you did,' interrupted Sharon my best friend. 'You had a turkey, remember.' She laughed as I smiled and nodded. She was right. My father had won a turkey in a raffle in a pub. He has only got a small fridge and it wouldn't hold the turkey so he saw my brother on the way from school and gave it to him.

Mary looked in disbelief. She didn't know whether to believe Sharon or not. I smiled at Sharon and was relieved that she had managed to get me out of a difficult situation. We went to our next lesson leaving Mary puzzled. We talked of a completely different subject, pretending to have forgotten the conversation.

You see people with married parents find it extremely difficult to comprehend life as 'a product of a broken marriage'. OK, they understand that your parents live apart and that you probably live with your mother, but that is as far as it goes. They innocently think that you see your father every weekend when he takes you out somewhere nice, that at Christmas and birthdays you get twice as many presents as before because both your parents are buying separately and that your mother gives you pocket money in the week and your father gives you some at the weekend – therefore you get two lots of money.

However, this is not true, especially not in my case and in most others, I suspect. I only see my father when I make the effort to walk uphill to his flat which takes three-quarters of an hour, even then when I get there, there is no guarantee that he will be in. I have no alternative then really but either to stand around outside waiting for him to come back here (probably at closing time which could be hours) or to go back home with a wasted journey.

Even when he is home, he doesn't seem to be particularly

161

pleased to see me – he makes more fuss over the dog. I don't expect a kiss or a hug because we've never been that close, just a simple 'how are you?' or 'it's nice to see you'. Then he either carries on doing what he was already doing, for example, planting tomato plants in seed trays (he grows tomato plants on his flat window sill) or just sits there and talks about Steve my brother. Soon he runs out of questions about him and frequently asks about my mother. At first he would say something like 'How is she now?' I'd answer and then he would say, 'It should never have happened – it wouldn't have it it wasn't for those bloody interfering relatives.'

I would sit there in silence whilst he brought up the fact that he had lent my uncle some money out of his redundancy pay and that's what helped him set up business – then he would start on my aunt – and anyone else he could think of. He would then continue with: 'I know every dimple on your mother's bum, you know.'

I'd just look at him and then finally about twenty minutes after I had arrived he would finish by saying, 'I suppose I'd better give you a lift home,' and he would.

He never once asked me how school was going, or even asked me what I was doing for that matter, he never offered me a drink or a biscuit and I was never once invited to stay for a meal.

That was my visit to my father's. Other times I went up there to borrow something, like on one occasion I wanted to borrow a flat cap I knew he had and didn't use for a play I was doing in school. During these visits I usually got really annoyed and came close to tears. I often left without the trivial item I had come for in the first place.

As soon as I got there I'd ask if I could borrow his cap please. He'd say 'Oh, er I don't think I can find it.' If I told him where it was he would go on about me being nosey and never missing anything. Then he would say, 'You never come to see me unless you want something.' I would start getting annoyed and say, 'I shouldn't have to walk all this way to see you anyway – you should come down to the house, pick up me and Steve and take us out.'

He'd say, 'Don't be daft, you know I'm not allowed in that house, your bastarding mother saw to that.'

'But you don't have to come inside, just pick us up.'

'I don't want to end up in jail. You know there's a court order. I can't take you anywhere anyway without your mother's permission!'

'All you have to say, Dad, is how about coming to town or somewhere and I'd ask Mum, who'd agree straightaway anyway.'

Tempers would get hot and he would start saying, 'Your mother was sleeping with a coon anyway. She slept with a f----g blackman. You know that, don't you?'

He would just go on and on and on. Of course I would try not to let this upset me but it would, although I knew there was no truth in his stupid allegations.

I can remember going to the beach one evening with mum, dad, Steve and Jacky who was an old friend of my mum's, who came on holiday with us and round for tea on Tuesdays, Thursdays and Sundays.

I can remember walking on the shore and thinking why did Dad and Jacky go to the pub at night and Mum stayed behind and looked after us.

I asked her innocently, 'Why is Dad always with Aunt Jacky?' My mother evaded the question. This must have made my mum realise that I was old enough to accept the situation and that she could put up with my father no longer. He wasn't having an affair with her or anything, he just neglected my mother and took her for granted – he didn't do his share in caring for me and Steve either.

163

One evening, a few months later, my mother came into my room and sat on my bed where I was lying and she said, 'Your father and I have been thinking – we've decided to get a divorce.'

I was dumbfounded. Yes, I knew divorce happened all the time and that even a few of my friends' parents were divorced like Sharon's, but not my parents. I knew that they had been arguing more lately but I had taken no notice and attached no importance to it.

My mother continued, 'It doesn't mean that we both don't love you and we both don't want you to think that it's your fault. You will have to decide later on who you want to live with.' Fighting back the tears she whispered, 'Your brother wants to stay with your father, but you make your own mind up.' She got up and went to the door.

'Mum,' I called, wiping the tears from my eyes, 'I want to stay with you.'

She smiled and relief spread across her face even though her eyes were still red and sore from crying.

This was the closest I had and have ever felt to my mother. I was slightly confused but before things got better they got worse. I understood what was happening but only as an eleven-year-old and not as I would have understood if I was older.

Before this Mum had had a fierce argument with Jacky accusing her of being with my father. Jacky left and didn't come round again.

Even now I am certain he wasn't having an affair as I've already said, but I agree that my mother had fair grounds for suspicion.

It took a year and a half for the divorce to actually come through and another year or so for my father to move out. This time was hell, it was the worst few years of my life. My father refused to move out after the divorce and my mother had to get a court order which took time. She kicked him out of the bedroom and he resorted to sleeping in the old car he kept in the garage and whenever he could he made a big deal about this to me. My mother refused to cook his meals and he cooked separately, usually trying to make us feel sorry for him by cooking pathetic meals. He often fried fish and liver in the same frying pan just to get sympathy — which, by the way, he rarely did receive because I wasn't as stupid as he thought.

When he moved out it was great for the first few weeks but then I began to miss him (after all he was still my father). He didn't come and see me so I used to visit him.

I still miss him but I don't visit any more.

MARIA MORRIS

Bodenham, Herefordshire

Well, there I was, stamping the name of our school onto the fly-leaves of a whole batch of books and what did I come across? A spanking new pile of crispy white paper, that's what. Actually, it wasn't really spanking new, in fact, judging by the layer of dust which buried it and the dejected way in which it sat in one corner of that jungle of a stockroom, I'd say it had been there a good few years. Well, being kind-hearted, I decided to take this lonely wad of whiteness into my care . . . and here it is, receiving the attention of my pen, but enough about that.

I've decided to dedicate my wild and crazy teenage thoughts to this loyal paper, so that I've got something to do while Mum and Dad are downstairs having a screaming match. I think *he's* come back to collect the rest of his

165

possessions, the ones he forgot to take with him last time he was round, and the time before and the time before that. I'd have thought he'd have got the message by now; Mum doesn't want him and neither do I. It's his own fault though, he brought it upon himself, I mean, would you be very happy with a dad who went and 'got acquainted' with another woman? And to think, he promised to love and cherish Mum, 'till death do us part'. But then all males of any description are the same, it's just that Dad went too far; he was always spending his money on things other than his family.

Some of my mates reckon that boys are the best things since sliced bread, whereas I tend to think of them as a bunch of showground poodles, with their permed hair and trendy Nike trainers, along with their personalised six-foot ghetto blasters.

Parents. Are they all like mine, or am I the only individual on the whole of this globe who has to suffer with parents that I don't understand? Why do they have to quarrel all the time, and over such trivial things too? When they were still together, they used to quibble over things like when they were going to go out, and where they should go, and 'What's wrong with having chips every other day?' (That would be my Dad, by the way.) Another thing that gets me about parents is that when they do finally decide where to go for our holiday, for example, it's usually somewhere like a fortnight in the Lake District, so there we are wandering through boggy marshland in the pouring rain, with nothing but miles and miles of 'beautiful' scenery to look at and the odd blank-faced sheep. I reckon that sheep aren't really that dumb, but the looks on their faces are really those of deep concentration, in fact they're probably thinking complicated philosophical thoughts like 'what is the algebraic equation of the percentage increase of Australian rainfall?' Or, 'what the hell are those fools doing, in boggy marshland in the pouring rain?'

I think I just heard the door slam. He's gone now, for good I hope. I bet you any money that at this very minute, Mum's sitting in the kitchen smoking cigarette after cigarette, without the slightest care in the world about what she's doing to her heart and lungs; but then her heart's ruined now anyway, it'll never repair.

I had a boyfriend once, you know, Never again. After him I wouldn't trust any male, even if he got down on one knee and thrust a bunch of rare and exotic orchids into my arms, knowing the likes of them round here, they'd probably be those plastic ones that squirt water at you through a little hole. I remember seeing a boy do that to his girlfriend once. He got down on one knee just like I said, sang a little verse, then held out these flowers to her and just as she was about to take them, he pressed a little round plastic thing and a jet of water flew out of the fair blossom and was she surprised! She flung her arms up in the air and went beserk: 'Scream, scream, scream!' she went! The end of another happy relationship. My boyfriend wasn't like that, though, I was lucky in that respect. No, my boyfriend was completely different. He was worse. It was good while it lasted though, I've got to admit. Those kisses, wow, those lip-smacking beauties were winners with me every time. I wonder what those other girls thought of his kisses? He must have had a full-time job on his hands, so that's why I decided to make life a little easier for the poor, poor dear. To be frank, I ditched the two-timing sod.

Exams bother me. Some people like my mate Jill revise till they're blue in the face . . . and pass. Others, like Cyrenna, for example, don't . . . and pass. I do both . . . and fail. I do one . . . and fail. I do the other . . . and fail.

167

What really gets me, is that no matter how hard I slog my guts out for my mum, she ends up going to the school. When my mum goes to the school, it bothers me. Hyperactive parents are always up to something.

I had a French exam yesterday. I sat there for the whole hour doodling on the corner of my desk and reading the etchings. One said, 'Here fell Jo Whitey, murdered by a computing paper no. one. 21/6/84'; another said, 'Sex is evil, evil is sin. Sin is forgotten so . . .' I couldn't read the rest of that one as it was a bit worn away. Shame. 'Pink Floyd' was intricately carved into the wood at one end of the desk, so I decided to add my own little doodle, to bring things up to date. With my compass, I scratched a bumble bee (which happens to be my personal mark), that is until my compass bust; then, just as I was trying to fix it, a teacher came up and looked right down his nose at me. He gave me one of those warning looks that are supposed to scare you, then walked away. I hate French though, and I hate those silly questions they give you in exams. It's all very well asking what direction the loo is, but when it comes to having an interesting conversation with a foreigner, you only ever get as far as talking about the state of the weather lately and can you have a croissant with plenty of mustard please? Then when I reach section B, question two, it turns out to be something like, 'Que fais-tu, Marie-Claude?' Who cares what she's doing, because I know I don't! She could be doing triple-back somersaults and I wouldn't bat an eyelid.

Usually, in lessons such as maths, I give up listening and practice the art of sleeping with my eyes open, which is pretty clever, if you can do it without the teacher jolting you back to consciousness; then you just have to fall on his mercy. 'You weren't paying attention, were you? No? I thought so. One day you'll regret it.' (I think I am already.)

168

'You'll be sorry, blah blah blah . . .' Then, by the time he's finished you've gone and nodded off again. But the trouble with teachers is that they reckon we're a bunch of thickies who are blind to the world. Only we know what is really going on though. To them, unemployment is a lack of jobs, while to us it is living on a few pounds' dole money, whether we have three 'A' levels in our pockets or not. To them, politics are the complicated rules, ways in which we must live and the matters of society that must be looked into, for the well-being of our country. To us, it is the garble that has made our life what it is today. It isn't The Teacher and The Pupil, or The Elders and Youth, it is Them v. Us.

Once, we had a really soft teacher, I think her name was Miss Brown or something. I remember that she was quite old, the strictly disciplined type, yet when it came to controlling a class of fifteen year olds, she turned into a dithering heap. For a start, Danny Pierce, like the childish fool he is, kept yelling out that he wanted to go for a pee, (you'd have thought he was toilet-trained by now) and then there were the boys at the back, who kept making weird noises, like faulty foghorns and sheep farting. (Why do I keep bringing sheep into this? Do sheep fart?) Well, after Danny had yelled, 'Wee wee!' for about the millionth time, the fire alarm went off. The whole class jumped up at the same time as chairs went flying everywhere and there was a mad rush of hysteria and people scrambling and climbing over each other to get to the door first. Meanwhile, Miss Brown was screeching, 'Naow children,' (she talked like that, did Miss Brown). 'Naow children, we must keep order and contain ourselves. We shall disperse quietly.' Then Danny said, or rather shouted, 'I think I already have!' Anyway, by the time most of us had reached the field for register callings, Miss Brown was still waving her arms about and going, 'Screech screech!' Any other teacher would have bellowed something like, 'Get a move on, you pack o' blinking morons!' It all turned out to be a false alarm in the end, because some jerk smashed the glass on one of those little red boxes (you know the type I mean) by accident, when he slung his bag over his shoulder. It annoys me when they do that, because if you're standing behind them at the time, you end up flat out on the floor, having received a left-hook from a Slazenger bag. Mostly the owner of the vicious bag doesn't even notice what's happened!

My pen's running out, not much left on the ol' clock. I need to buy one. I need cash. I need a job, a part-time job. The thing is, most jobs for people in school are pretty long hours, with small pay, like a newspaper round for example. Every morning you rub your bleary eyes and set off into the rising sun, brave the blizzards, the gales, the torrential downpours. You pole-vault over gates that won't open, fight with fierce dogs and battle with vicious letter boxes. Then when the morning lies are delivered you return to base, mission accomplished, to receive your reward; five old and grubby notes (and in case you're wondering, they're not tenners). That's it in a nutshell really. If however, you want to sweep the floor and lug all the heavy boxes around in a shop, then fine. If you've got a mathematical brain and are not the sort who gives three-quid change from a fifty-pence piece, then I'm sure you'll go far on a till. Or maybe you could work in a pub, pulling pints and picking up the peanuts off the floor, that is if you can bear holding conversations on fly-fishing, listening to people's views on the present figures in the stock exchange and ignoring the sideways glances to certain parts of your anatomy from a group of shifty-looking old men. But enough about jobs. The subject's simply too depressing.

170

Have any of you fellow girls out there noticed how hard it is to please other people? We're always expected to have twenty-two inch waists which leads to the problem of food. You starve yourself to skin and bone or live on a diet of muesli and carrot juice, you can choose from the wide variety of healthy foods. Picture the scene: you shift your weight (all fourteen stone of it) back and forth along the shelves. Will you have the cardboard flakes (bran crisps), bath sponge sprinkled with scouring powder (lowfat cake with special diet sugar), or will it be a few slices of granite rock, with axle-grease (crispy wholemeal bread with extra healthy margarine)? You're spoilt for choice so buy a Mars bar instead. If you ever manage to obtain the waistline desired, then you are faced with the problem of what type of clothes you should wear. A Littlewood's number bought in the sale is no good, I'm afraid. The main rules are, that they must have a designer label; this is one of the essential ingredients – Lacoste or some other nifty label like Benetton or Pepe. Failing that, you could always pop down to the local jumble sale, which is one of the really hip places to go. But honestly, I remember when if you wore something from a jumble sale, you'd be the laughing stock of the neighbourhood; if you decided to hit the town with whatever number you bought, you'd find that your friends suddenly didn't want to know you: 'Who's she?'

'It's me, your bestest ever pal!'

'Ha ha, very funny. Look, if you don't beat it then you'll be in trouble.'

'B. . b. . but . . .'

'You heard, now hop it, and take your purple flares with you.'

Sad isn't it? These days it's all cardigans on your head (worn as a supposedly very trendy hat), leggings round your neck and shoes on your hands. Ah well, that's life.

My pen's nearly died now, so I'll wrap a pair of leggings round my neck, have a quick swig of the ol' carrot juice and see if the sheep in the Lake District can tell me where I can find a job.

DRUGS ◄

Southsea, Hampshire

My story of my teenage years is not one I am proud of and my greatest wish would be to turn the clock back.

When I was fifteen I went to live with my mother; my parents had divorced. It was a big upheaval and with being the 'new girl' at school, I found it very difficult to fit in. Everyone else had been friends for years and I felt very left out. A friend of my mother's owned a café and let me work there on Saturdays and school holidays. It was hard work, but I enjoyed working there and soon got to know the regulars.

There was one group of so-called 'hippies' who came in most days. Their way of life appealed to me, unconventional and free. They were very friendly and I was desperately short of friends. I went out of my way to talk with them and was rewarded with being asked to their house after work. The house was quite dirty, obviously a duster and Hoover were not part of their belongings, but the atmosphere was warm, I felt at ease with them, but at the same time quiet and in awe of them. After the first time of going round, I frequently went. It was so different to being left out at school. I felt wanted. To make them like me more, I took food round there – left-overs from the café – and cleaned up the place for them (although every time I went it was back to normal).

They all smoked cannabis, so I joined in. I couldn't afford not to. I did not want to be different. I did not particularly like the effect of the drug; it made me feel tired and hungry, but I continued to smoke it. I had to.

Sex was another thing I felt I should do. I wasn't a virgin, but had had little sexual experience. John, one of the lads who lived at the house, was interested in me, so I started going to bed with him. We rarely dated, we just went with each other when we saw each other. I didn't particularly like John, but in a way I used him, to make sure I was accepted.

One evening, when I went round to the house, only Chris was in. He was, in a way, the leader. We chatted and smoked cannabis, then he started kissing me. I knew what the outcome would be, but by making out with him, I knew that I really was accepted.

I continued to see John and make out with Chris occasionally. John knew about Chris, but wasn't bothered. John and I finished after a couple of weeks and I started to see another lad, known as Scouse. By this time I had made out with about five lads who went round there.

I was still at school, but my past ambition to be a teacher had gone. I was eager to leave both home and school. My mother was fairly strict about the amount of times I went out and I had to be in by 10.30.

When I was seventeen I left school to work in a shop and shortly afterwards, I left home to live in a bedsit. It was damp and grotty, but mine. I loved it. Six months later, I left the shop to work in a factory: here were two jobs I had always vowed I would never do.

During that six months quite a lot had happened at the 'hippy house'. Other drugs were being introduced, new faces were coming in and old ones had left. I did not like heroin being around. It scared me. But I did get a good deal of fun out of the amphetamines. They made me feel good, an extra buzz. We would shoot speed, then go to a disco, come back still wide-awake and play cards until dawn. Pointless really, looking back.

I had stopped sleeping around by now, realising I did not need to, to become accepted. The older girls in the group did not. I thought they had, and had tried to be like them. I had made a few good girlfriends, which was what I had really wanted.

I had noticed, at the discos, a heroin dealer watching me a lot. His name was Paul, and I was very flattered. Everybody was always looking for Paul, with him dealing, yet he was interested in me. I played hard to get for a month or so. He kept chatting me up, but I kept my distance, yet at the same time doing my utmost to keep him interested. One week, he approached me and said he would be in town the next day and could he come round? I agreed. By this time I had moved from the grotty bedsit to a flat. It was lovely, spacious and clean. I was very nervous of Paul coming and spent the whole day tidying and cleaning. I had given up hope of him coming round, when at 8.30 there was a knock at the door. Paul stood there with a friend. I invited them in and went to make a cup of tea. Paul followed me, apologising for bringing his friend, saying he couldn't get rid of him. Then he asked me for a couple of spoons and two glasses of water. When I returned to the front room with the tea, I found them preparing heroin to inject. Paul offered me some, but I refused. After they had all had their turn, Paul again offered me some. I just said no, I didn't know what else to say. I did not want him to think I had not ever had it before, but he guessed, so I admitted I had not. He then measured a small amount out for me, saying I would enjoy it. He did not force me to, but I felt he would think me a child if I did not. Heroin frightened, yet fascinated me. I was dumbstruck as he inserted the needle into my vein.

Soon afterwards, his friend left. Paul and I chatted, in between my being sick. The heroin was not all it was cracked up to be. Paul said it was always like that the first time. I found out that he had recently split up with his

177

girlfriend and was looking for a place. At present he was staying with a friend but obviously couldn't stay there for ever. That night Paul and I slept together and from then on he stayed. He said it would only be for a couple of weeks, just until he found a place of his own.

During the next few weeks I found out what being a heroin dealer really meant. It meant people calling round at all times, night and day, having to unplug the phone to stop it ringing, people staying the night, expecting to be fed and having no time to yourself. I was also expected to clean up, keep everything tidy. Paul was a perfectionist. He was also a junkie and violent. He hit me several times, not caring if others were there or not. It was always for something petty, like not warming his dinner plate.

It was obvious our relationship was not built to last. I never had really expected it to, but Paul had not even begun to look for anywhere. As time went on, I was increasingly scared of him. His temper was worsening. Although drugs were probably part of the reason, I found out that he was naturally violent. He had a whole string of convictions for football hooliganism, mugging, shoplifting and much more. I was too scared to ask him to leave. This went on for about six months.

The one good thing about him was he never let me get to be a heroin addict, but then the more he gave me, the less profit he would have made. I doubt if it was out of concern for me. For the next few months I rarely went out. I saw little of the friends I had tried so hard to gain. They were part of the old crowd, that had gradually moved away from the heroin scene.

The final straw came at Christmas. Paul had not even bothered to buy me a present. It upset me that he thought that little of me. His beating me up, splitting my lips, giving me bloody noses and black eyes, plus numerous bruises – I was rarely without them – was bad enough, but now . . . While Paul was out, I got my case and packed. I had no idea where I was going, and realised that I would be leaving behind my wonderful flat and furniture that I'd worked hard to achieve. I did not care. To be rid of Paul I would have given anything.

Suddenly the door opened and Paul walked in. I froze. He asked what I was doing. I told him I had had enough, I could no longer live with him. He then sat down and seemed stunned. He cried, said he was sorry, but I had heard it all before, all too frequently, after his violent outbursts. Suddenly (it was always sudden), he started hitting me, all over. It was as if he was in a frenzy. Then he jumped up, ran to the kitchen, returning with an iron. I know the meaning of 'scared stiff' now, for I could not move for fear. He struck me with it, I lost count of the number of times, on my legs, arms and ribs. At one stage, I can remember managing to pull the iron out of his hands; the only thing that stopped me from putting it through his skull, was in case I did *not* kill him – what would he do to me? The moment was gone and he had snatched it back. He ran shouting through the flat and I used my chance to escape, running wildly to the corner café. They let me through to the back, telephoned an ambulance and the police, after I explained what had happened.

That was the last time I ever saw Paul. When the ambulance came I could hardly walk, and I realised how sheer fear can make you overcome pain. It was found I had no broken bones, Paul had not hit me hard enough, which made it worse. It meant it could not have been a real frenzy, he had calculated how hard he hit me. He knew what he was doing. After that I moved to my father's, three hundred miles away. I had to get away.

Paul was sentenced to six months in prison. I was scared

of what might happen, when he was back in town. I thought he might try to kill me.

Now I'm trying to build a new life for myself and my daughter. I found out I was pregnant soon after moving. I did feel tempted to let Paul know, but it would not have been worth it. I think it is better for my daughter never to know him.

It's been difficult. After living with drugs and that life-style, no matter how bad the experience, it's hard to fit into the 'job, mortgage, husband' ideals, though I want to want them very much.

If anyone is willing to take advice, mine is simple – if he hits you, even just once, leave him. It may end in death – my experience very nearly did. And as to drugs, forget them. They are a hell of a lot worse than the worst that is said of them.

THE FUTURE ◄

'KAREN McCARTHY'

Chelmsford, Essex

I have just seen *My Brilliant Career* for the sixth time. I replay the videos again and again, painfully involved in Harry's quest for Sybilla and her quest for fulfilment in her most brilliant of careers. I feel close to Sybilla. I, too, am a plain precocious girl, with a tongue too sharp for my own good and little else to distinguish me from a crowd. I, too, want a career, but this is the 1980s not the 1890s and a career seems further away even than it was for a plain Australian girl. This plain English girl is facing a future of unemployment, crime problems, falling living standards and the ever-present threat of destruction. I want to be special. I need to be special. I can't settle for a life on the dole. Girls in my class who want to be typists and house-wives do nothing but confirm my belief that I'll die if I ever become like them.

Life in the 1980s. Let me start with my school. The best years of your life. Only schoolteachers say that. My school is killing me. They don't poison my food or booby trap my desk, but they keep me down, stifling and suffocating me. I sit in maths and I can't see the sense of it. Will I find happiness square-rooting the number of unemployed, turning the number of closed hospitals into a quadratic equation? So I sit and dream. I dream of films and plays, of being an actress. That way I can become another person, more lively, more intelligent, more beautiful than I am. I need that. Getting away is all I want.

This picture of my life wouldn't be complete without a mention of heroes. The 1980s are a come-back for the heroes of Saturday morning movies. Indiana Jones is who I want to be. I want to be carefree and adventurous. Then I remember what I am, what I look like, what I think and feel. Film heroes help me to escape from what I am, they lift me out of my skin. They're safe for me to love, they won't let me down, they have all the qualities I don't. Emilio Estevez smoulders at me through the celluloid. Mel Gibson gazes longingly at me, as I sit stuffing my dull, everyday face with popcorn, telling them that I'll soon be there.

So I sit writing about the beginning of my life. In my safe house, in my safe country town. One day I'll get out. I'll be special, until then I can only write about how great I am. My great work of fiction. I won't show this to my parents. I can't tell them about my secret life. In these times, it's embarrassing to admit to ambition, to admit to wanting more out of life, to being dissatisfied with what I've got. I feel that I can't tell them that I don't want to be like them. I love them but I'm not like them.

I'm glad that I'm alive, despite all the things that I hate about myself. If I have talent, I may fit in in spite of myself, my looks and my tendency to look on the dark side. I hope I have talent, I want someone to tell me that I have, to reassure me. I often wonder if it's worth it. I find myself asking that question more and more. If I live to be fifty, it's what I'll remember most about this time. That terrible feeling that you'll never be anything, that you'll be one of the faceless thousands that remind you of what's really going to happen.

This decade has given me a lot, my ambition to be somebody. Perhaps it's the feeling of depression that makes me determined to come out of it better than anyone else. If I don't succeed, I don't know if it'll be because of me or because of the rest of the world, but I know I'll make it through this decade. I've already decided what I want to do, where I'm going, what I think of myself. This is the start

184

of my personal, ambitious, brilliant (?) career. It may end with the 1980s, too, but I'll have had a try at being something special.

VICKIE ORTON ◀

Great Shelford, Cambridgeshire

I am a teenager of the 1980s which means that I'm a product of the 1960s. Whilst my parents were busy making love not war, they are now part of a society which wants to ban abortion and confidential contraception for the under-sixteens.

The 1980s are the anti-climax of the 1960s and early 1970s. It's not that everything's been done but that the money to do it with has gone. No really new fashions have taken off in the 1980s (ironically, there was a swing back to the fifties and sixties) but technology has. Computers and videos have become assumed household objects, but they are also putting people out of work; a decision has to be made between people and machines or else a whole new lifestyle must be created.

The decline we see in the 1980s began in the late 1970s. The punks of the seventies knew this and tried to rebel with loud music, outlandish clothes and hairstyles. Ideally, a state of anarchy should have arisen but things went wrong. Punk heroes, the Sex Pistols, became multi-millionaires, as did those dealing with them. Suddenly punk became big business, punk clothes, once a cheap innovation, became designer clothes costing a packet from trendy boutiques. Punk, once a form of self-expression against the rat race and everything it stood for, became a great contributor to the capitalist society. For some people, it was a deliberate move up the social ladder.

At the start of the 1980s new hope was expressed by the new romantics with their frilly shirts and electronic music. They themselves didn't last long; like the punks they moved on to better things, but they did leave a trademark. That trademark still exists today and probably will do until somebody thinks to rebel against it. It is the trademark of image. There has been no really new pop music in the eighties because pop groups are signed up for their looks and not their sounds. Image has played an important role in the eighties, and not just for its youth. A slim, health food freak is the desired image at the moment; everything is 'half the fat but all the taste'.

It's a popular trend for teenagers to dress in black, symbolically in mourning for life. Whilst 1960s fashions are borrowed, the bubble isn't there. We are more mature than the flower children of the sixties. The musical *Hair* is now a joke, as sex has been brought out into the open, perhaps due to the sixties. Socialism no longer rules; people are swinging to the 'middle of the road' with the advent of the SDP-Liberal Alliance, and Thatcherism, formerly Conservatism, is a dangerous thing to practice.

We are the angry youth, we want work. People realise that demonstrations don't work; there is now more violence on the streets. Petty and major crime are on the increase. There is very little going for the youth of today. Many people have lost faith in society, even the police have been discovered to have criminal tendencies. Police shootings of innocent people are commonplace.

There is hope in the eighties and there are jobs, too, but they are in the south. The south itself is no golden land but things are better. Things seem to suddenly change when you reach the south. Academic standards are higher; people do have an incentive, people are healthier, even the weather is better.

My life in the eighties took a dramatic change when I suddenly moved from the depressed north of Glasgow to the affluent Cambridge. It was as though I'd been suffering from a great sickness, indeed many traits of which will remain with me throughout my life. A slogan had been devised in Glasgow proclaiming that 'Glasgow is miles better', but as the Glasgow university rag mag pointed out, Glasgow is the only city to be ill in the first place. The people of Glasgow have been suffering from an illness, that of despondency with the added condition of nationalism. It was not until I moved away that I realised how bad that sickness was. I have an enormous chip on my shoulder about wealth, everything I buy must be justified. Previously, I believed that everybody held such an attitude, but in the south it's different. People talk about unemployment and poverty but they don't really understand what they are talking about. I was given new hope when I moved to the south; I managed to get a job and a place at college to do 'A' levels. Like so many people in the north, I thought I was useless, I saw little point in staying on at school if I was only going to go on the dole afterwards. Teachers did little to dispel this attitude up north. Indeed their strike action just encouraged such attitudes.

Just because people in the north are despondent it doesn't mean that they don't care. The long and bitter miners' strike aroused most sympathy from those in need of help themselves. People in the north saw it as another blight caused by Thatcherism. By showing their support for the miners they were demonstrating against Thatcher. Also, many of the miners were in the already deprived north. Once again, controversy about the police was

187

aroused by the miners' action. However, public sympathy was also shifted away from the miners, as 'scabs' (working miners) were seriously injured or killed. This violence was extended to entire families by entire families. In those mines still open, such conflict still exists. However the miners did not win; Mrs Thatcher, the Iron Lady, still rules with a rod of iron.

It would be interesting to know the northerners' views on apartheid; certainly racial prejudice was strong in Scotland but the song, 'Free Nelson Mandela', was also very popular. In the south, people were angry with Thatcher and demanded sanctions (and imposed their own) but to no avail. The population was strongly against apartheid even if the government was not.

In the north, people were more violent. It is mainly the south who see the armed forces as fascists. CND was less strong in the north, but I did live eight miles from Faslane nuclear submarine base and what employment there was from there, so it was a natural reaction to the fear of losing work. Now I live surrounded by American airforce bases near Sizewell nuclear power station. There is a strong anti-American feeling here, especially after America bombed Libya from our bases. Even the people who live and work at Sizewell are prepared to protest against it and its further development. Indeed, it took the Soviet Chernobyl disaster to bring home the truth of our own nuclear reactors.

The eighties have lessened the class structure by making everybody middle-class but introducing extremes within the middle class. I am middle-class but I cannot rebel against this, because my parents were working-class and I have watched them climb up the social ladder. I don't like being middle-class, it doesn't fit my instincts but there is nothing I can do about it, and it has after all brought me a future. Like all teenagers I long to leave home but lack of money and work make it difficult. I am from a generation which is not at ease with our parents, not because of their strictness but because of their success.

The 1980s delivered a generation old before their time, carrying the worries of the world. It brought tension between the north and the south which will no doubt explode in the 1990s. But we will have left home by then.

HELEN MINSHALL

Loughborough, Leicestershire

Grown-ups say to us we've never had it so good. They give us lectures about how, when they were teenagers, they had to leave school and start work in order to bring more money into the family. They never had as much pocket money, couldn't go to youth clubs or to the cinema; they really seem to believe that life is far easier for teenagers today.

Well, are things easier? OK, most teenagers get a fairly reasonable amount of pocket money, more than their parents did, but I don't think it buys all that much more. Teenagers can afford to go to the cinema as a treat every so often and there are lots of youth clubs and other organisations to join. But does this add up to a better life for us?

At fifteen, if I go to my local youth club my parents insist on meeting me out afterwards because it is in a very rough area. Fear is something we all feel a lot these days. How many places are there where it is completely safe to walk alone at night? I believe we live in a very violent age. However, the fear of being attacked by someone is a relatively minor fear when compared to the fear of a nuclear

189

war. We have not had a world war for over forty years, although we are still reminded of the last war nearly every day.

Now the superpowers think it is necessary to produce nuclear weapons as 'protection'. Well, I don't think they are much use as 'protection' when, if one reactor catches fire, it affects millions of people with radiation poisoning. All it needs now is for there to be one argument between the two superpowers and a nuclear war may start, which would end the world as we know it.

Of course the general public are never consulted before governments go ahead to produce nuclear weapons. Although not everyone supports CND (Campaign for Nuclear Disarmament) I think the majority of us would prefer not to be involved with nuclear power for safety reasons alone. At first, nuclear power was thought to be a very cheap method of producing energy, however, I don't think that the side-effects of radiation poisoning come cheaply!

Why is there so much demand for fuel and energy in the world today? The more fuel we use, the more polluted our environment becomes. We should try to cut down on the amount of fuel we use, and be more concerned about conservation. For a start, there are too many cars on the road today. It is amazing that so many people use their cars to travel even the shortest journeys. Surely it is better to walk or cycle if the distance is not too great. This not only helps with the amount of fuel but also does our bodies more good.

As it seems that there is an ever-increasing need for energy I think we should explore the possibilities of using new methods, such as solar and tidal power. These, I believe, will be much safer than nuclear power, and will be unlikely to run out as present fuel like coal will do soon.

Now that society is becoming more industrialised, it seems that there are fewer jobs. There will be a time when machines can take over all jobs! The problem of high unemployment is very severe at the moment. This means prospects do not look very promising for us teenagers. It seems that you need more and more qualifications in order to succeed in getting a job. This puts so much pressure on us that is is not surprising that 40 per cent of teenagers taking 'O' levels fail.

Education is becoming more and more important in today's society. This happens at a time when the government cuts down on spending in schools! What chance does that give us of getting good exam results when we miss school as teachers strike over low pay? Is it any wonder that so many people leave school at sixteen with hardly any qualifications and join the never-ending dole queue?

There is a lot wrong with the world today, not just in Britain but all over the world. At least half of all Third World countries are in such poverty that millions of people in these countries are starving. Charity events staged in richer countries have raised several millions of pounds to help the Third World countries, but sadly this is not enough. What is needed is for all the countries of the world to unite, and share out their wealth to the poorer countries, to give them long-term help. It is unfair that some countries have so much wealth while others have little or none: 'God provided enough for every man's need but not for every man's greed!'

Politics also contributes a lot towards hardship in the world today. The apartheid system in South Africa means that black people are second-class citizens. It is bad enough that we have racial prejudice in England, but at least there are laws to prevent racial discrimination. In South Africa racial prejudice is the law – employers must employ white

191

people before black people. Those who speak out against apartheid are locked up indefinitely as political prisoners. When riots escalate the government introduces a state of emergency tactic, which means the police can use any amount of force against offenders; foreign journalists and newscasters can be arrested for witnessing and recording violence; and anyone who makes subversive comments against apartheid can also be arrested.

Sadly, there is very little that we, as outsiders, can do to stop apartheid. If we employ sanctions against South Africa, how can we be sure these will not make things worse for the black people we're trying to help? For instance, if we stop importing gold from South Africa, mines will have to close down, black workers will lose their jobs and they will have less money to look after their families.

A problem facing youngsters in England and other rich countries today is drugs. Legal drugs such as tobacco and alcohol already cause so much damage to our bodies that the NHS wastes thousands of pounds each year repairing 'self-inflicted' damage to people's bodies caused by too much alcohol or tobacco. Now there are much worse drugs on the market such as LSD, cannabis, cocaine and the worst of all – heroin. Drug-pushers earn their living, a very decent living, by indirectly ruining the lives of youngsters. It is time that kids were taught at an early age what drugs do to them. Perhaps if they realise this, they might have the strength to refuse any drugs offered to them. It would be great if the in-thing was to say 'no' to drugs, but sadly it isn't. It is far easier to accept than to refuse drugs.

It seems that there is little left that is right in the world today. We have all the problems of drugs, apartheid, poverty in Third World countries, unemployment, fuel use and nuclear power. However, if we take this negative attitude to blaming others and doing nothing to solve the problems then, of course, the problems will not be solved.

It is good that there are already so many organisations concerned with the problems of the world. We must join these organisations, make them stronger, and thus more able to actively help to solve the problems.

I believe that we are the generation who are most able to help save the world. We must finally do something to save our world from destruction by the many forces of evil. As a Christian, I believe that if there was more trust in God, there would be fewer problems in the world today. We must pull our resources together and make our world good and fair once more before it is too late – the hand is already hovering over the nuclear war button which could end the world!

SARAH EBNER

Kenton, Middlesex

It was my birthday and I was wondering what I should buy with my birthday money. Eventually I decided on a real treat: a video-cassette. 'I have wanted one for ages,' I told mum happily. As the conversation progressed, Mum told me what she had considered a real luxury when she was younger. To my surprise it was a record. 'I asked my very closest friends to buy me a record for my twenty-first birthday,' she told me.

Nowadays, I know that an album is a brilliant present (my best friend bought me the new Queen album for my birthday and I was really pleased with it), but for one of the most important birthdays in one's life, and from one's most special friend, I am sure that we would not consider an album as a really, really special present nowadays.

We may have more material things, but the worst thing about being a teenager and living in these times is the reputation which we teenagers as a whole have obtained. The muggings, rapes and murders which have become a daily occurence are blamed, often with justification, on us. However, give us a chance. Who do we blame? Are we all blameless? Or do we stand together sharing the faults which cause these atrocities? I personally believe that, yes, television is responsible, perhaps not totally, but certainly for a part. How is it that nowadays, when even very young children are able to watch all the sex and violence that is shown on the televison, many more crimes are committed? Thirty-five years ago, when many fewer people had television, and even if they did, they did not watch it as much as people do nowadays, many fewer crimes were committed. This can be verified by facts and figures. It is quite definitely a fact.

Politics plays a much more direct part in our lives than they did for our older equivalents. Most of my friends have some type of political views, whether they are trendy lefties or fascists. So as not to make any enemies, I won't state my political views here. Let's just say that I don't support CND or Red Wedge.

A problem that exists in our 'modern' society, and one that we should be speedily rid of, is the problem of racism (and anti-semitism). This problem does not seem to be as severe among the youth as it does among the older generations. Admittedly there are still National Front supporters among people in their early twenties, but I notice more racist remarks being said by (especially) OAPS. Steps are being taken to overcome the problem. However, some

194

people find great difficulty in not believing that all Irish or black people are stupid. Certainly, all Jewish people have long noses, and haven't you seen their horns . . .?

Music has quite definitely progressed over the years. Nowadays, every song must be accompanied by a hard-hitting video. Some groups originally get noticed not by their song but by their video. Take a very recent example. A-Ha, arguably the most popular new pop group. But wait, their first big hit, 'Take On Me', was released three times before it became a hit. The third time it was released, the song was accompanied by a quite brilliant video. Thus it appeared on all pop TV shows. 'Take On Me' was the ninth best-selling record in Britain last year.

At my local youth group last week, we had a discussion about the most important things in our lives today. 'What are you most proud of?' we were asked. We argued for most of the evening. The people who were proud to be teenagers were baffled. 'But everybody here is a teenager, why aren't you all proud of the fact?'

'They are the best years of your life, everybody is always saying that they wished they were young again.'

We argued non-stop. Were we proud to be teenagers or were we embarrassed to admit it? And the great debate continues. Are all teenagers 'wicked'? Should we get annoyed when our elders start to discuss the 'good old days'? Or will we be like them, pretending that the time when we lived was better, for nothing bad used to happen then, did it . . .?

I enjoy my life today. At the risk of being labelled forever a swot, I will honestly say that I would hate to leave school at the age of fourteen; I would hate not to at least have the chance to go on to higher education. I enjoy school, I enjoy exercising my brain, and I enjoy being able to make lasting friendships. Admittedly, there is a lot of pressure over

195

exams and, admittedly, I get totally neurotic over them, but I really do feel that I would not prefer to be out working for a living just yet. In my grandfather's time, however, I would have been.

Thus, at the tender age of fifteen, I am enjoying my life. I know that there will always be pressures which will never cease, but I have as much freedom now as I will ever have. I'm going to take my chances and, hopefully, succeed.

NAOMI RICHARDSON

Diss, Norfolk

Put your hand up if you need time to think. Not a very good response at all. Some of you can't hear me, some can't understand me and others, as usual, aren't even here. It's really a very simple question and I only want a simple answer.

We don't know how to think. It's something they left out of our education and so, presumably, we'll never know – pity that, but it can't be helped. We, being only human, like to huddle together and choose a few mindless people to be our leaders. We are content to follow them blindly and they really like the way we do that. They don't think, so why should we? Besides, look at the people who claim to think – all of them are religious maniacs or lunatics.

We don't like being told that we can't think. It makes us feel uneasy and stupid, so we collectively reject what you are saying and won't believe a word and refuse to discuss the matter. You keep on forgetting that we're British and proud of it. Just look at us. We haven't thought for generations and we're not going to start now.

I am at school and am learning how to be intelligent and intellectual. It's hard work but I don't mind because hard work is good for me. I am doing 'A' levels (what are 'A' levels? Can you eat them or do they help you get to sleep?). I have already got some splendid 'O' levels and my main aim is to get to a decent university and get myself a BA. Until then I am happy reading about Charles Dickens and doing geography projects. I don't work all the time so don't get the idea that I'm boring, I like to go out and broaden my mind, meeting interesting people, doing interesting things like finding out about the origins of French Post-Impressionism by visiting the National Gallery. I think that you will find that many people live interesting lives like me, but we still haven't learnt how to think.

Despite the fact that we can't think, you have to admit that *Homo Sapiens* is pretty ingenious, we build little thinks which can destroy huge things, call them bombs and use them to accumulate power. What do we do with the power we can wield? Well, we give it away to people we don't know, let alone trust. Take a look at the wretched 'middle class'. I loathe the middle class. It is deadly poisonous in the most charming way. We all love the pleasant, euphoric smell of conformity, remaining individuals but sharing the same morals and values and we all work for the same ultimate goal: comfort. It comes in all categories but is always the sweeter if it is well-deserved. No Englishman loves his cottage more than if he knows that he worked hard for it. Comfort is the Middle Man's dream but it rarely extends beyond the material. Comfort of mind is a subject few believe in and even fewer have. We can easily bury the deficiency by getting our friendly GP to prescribe a little something or we can say that our souls don't really exist and that it's weird to think of anything

197

beyond our broadsheet newspaper. Well, eat your toast and retire to Norfolk.

Some of us really do try to think. We all build our own happy little utopias where there is only ever room for the specially selected to live. We have nice little theories about being terribly nice to the terribly nice people we meet and all having a lot of fun because everybody is co-operating and helping each other but only if we belong to the group. Other people like to separate themselves and try to become perfect alone but rarely meet with success. So we are left with effort, not much but better than nothing. Let's face the problem we are in, ignoring words like: efficiency, profit and authority.

We are a selfish mean society, giving only to those who can afford, helping people who can return the assistance in our little moments of need. We forget things which are not in our immediate surroundings and even dare say that they do not exist until they happen to affect our tidy, tiny lives. We only love the people who love us and give time to people when we consider that we have a little to spare. We only live once so – 'Go For It'.

Please look for one moment at the world we live in. It is scared of living, not daring to object, subject to the greed and cruelty of the elite few who rule this ageing planet and everywhere there is misery, suffering, pain and fear. Does anyone disagree?

Where is your shame? It was sold in your quest for a logical mind. Where is your pity? You have become tired of the famine photos. Do you have any sympathy? Yes, but it got used up when we watched *The Color Purple*. We blame the education system, then we blame the government, but we never blame ourselves. Us? We're only mild-minded little humans who are weak and innocent. Mild but not blind, not until we choose to close our eyes and push our way through the establishment, regardless of the damage, faults, mistakes and errors, blindly following people we thought succeeded in life. Everything is Go, Go, Go. We rest by trying to push against the tide, by being a rebel, by growing suspicious plants in unseen places, but the return is inevitable. It is our cosy lives, our 'Be Best' orientated minds that can only produce the dilemma we live in. We are to blame; we are guilty.

There are social pressures, economic pressures, political pressures and, often, nagging, emotional pressures. This doesn't include physical pressures and with all that, we just don't have time to contemplate anything spiritual. Not today, thank you. I'm not interested in finding out how I really feel today, I don't want to know whether I live or merely exist. Didn't I tell you, I've got a geography project to do? Ha! If God really exists why doesn't he sort out the muddle the world is in. How did the world get to be such a tip anyway, especially if it started off being perfect? I can't think why. I can't think.

People are watching us all the time. We are their next unemployment figures, vote-holders and other terrible things. We will destroy our bit and then fade into the insignificance of the latest history books but not without teaching our principles to the ones who will follow us so that they can continue our obsolete way of existing, and we will be able to watch them trundle round in pointless circles as we did. The situation appears to be hopeless and helpless. But stop!

But wait! Time is graciously waiting for the People of the Eighties. For Us? Are we really that special, really that honoured and privileged? No, not at all, but the time has come. The time has come to turn 'Wogan' off, to sell the 'XR3i', to scrape the grimy make-up off, to return the filthy videos, to send 'Dallas' back to the pit it came from, to devour the last packet of Beef 'n' Tomato crisps, put the cover on the computer, get rid of the School of Thought they call intelligence and burn all our school textbooks. The time has come for us to sit down, close our eyes and think.

LAURI OWENS

Nailsea, Avon

One Thought

Six years ago, I fell on my stomach
I buried my face deep in sugar grass
was knotted with baby warm contentment,
smoothed my hair, clutched my face and laughed.
I peep at that fragment of memory,
I loved myself guiltlessly, my peach life.
At ten, you don't analyse emotions.
Sixteen, I live already in the past.